Advance praise for *The 5-Min··· ·*

"*The 5-Minute Healer* ··· ···aling
traditions. Capone an··· ··· ···f
knowledge, experience ··· ···is
extraordinary guide, wl··· ···mple, heart-
centered techniques for ··· ···ng. Their insight, straight-
forward approach and loving touch help the reader to shift
behaviors from those leading to stress and ill-health to those
that promote life, energy, joy and peace."
— Woody Vaspra and Catie Johnson,
co-founder, World Council of Elders

"In a time when many authors proffer shamanistic knowledge,
Jan Rupp knows of this terrain first hand. A healer of the
highest integrity, Jan's deep knowing is of rare value to those
desiring soul nurturance." —Peter A. Levine, PhD, author of
Waking the Tiger: Healing Trauma

"The welcoming message of this wonderful collaborative
effort is to keep it simple, rest deeper, and trust more fully in
our inherent intelligence for self-healing—whatever amount
of time we have." —Vickie Dodd, author of
Tuning the Blues to Gold: Soundprints

"This little book will serve as a convenient and much-needed
reminder of how to tune into ourselves—in whichever ways
work best for us—so we can help ourselves return to a more
calm or connected state of mind. What a wonderful resource!"
—Dr. Ellen Maslow, psychotherapist

"I have the great privilege of knowing Jan Rupp's work personally. I have found her depth of knowledge in a vast number of modalities to be extremely effective. She has so many windows of wisdom to look through that it is guaranteed to lead to clarity and a clear course of action. This well-composed book gives an insightful overview that will be helpful to the neophyte as well as the experienced practitioner. A must read for those taking responsibility for their own healing!"   —Diane Poole Heller, author of
A Self-Healing Guide to Auto Accident Trauma and Recovery

"I have used the *5-Minute Healer: Self-Healing Techniques for Busy People* both professionally and personally. As a clinical practitioner who treats both pre- and post-operative conditions, I highly recommend it for health care workers, their patients and all who provide human services. Capone and Rupp have captured the essence of many valuable self-healing techniques in ten concise and effective chapters. They describe each technique and offer exercises that are easily understood and implemented. *The 5-Minute Healer* provides the vehicle to achieve a happy, stress-free life, which in itself includes the miracle of recovery."   —Dr. Julie M. Artigliere, speech and language pathologist

The 5-Minute Healer

The 5-Minute Healer

Self-Healing Techniques for Busy People

Mary Capone & Janet Rupp

Johnson Books

BOULDER

Published by Johnson Books, a division of Johnson Publishing Company, 1880 South 57th Court, Boulder, Colorado 80301. E-mail: books@jpcolorado.com.

9 8 7 6 5 4 3 2 1

Cover design by Suzanne Sarto
Cover and text illustrations by Benko PhotoGraphics

Library of Congress Cataloging-in-Publication Data
Capone, Mary.
    The 5 minute healer: self-healing techniques for busy people / Mary Capone & Janet Rupp.
            p. cm.
Includes bibliographical references (p.   ).
    ISBN 1-55566-277-3
    1. Self-help techniques. I. Title: Five minute healer. II. Rupp, Janet. III. Title.
    BF632 .C363 2002
    158.1—dc21   2002013081

Printed in the United States

Contents

Preface

WE WROTE THIS BOOK to help people navigate the challenges of living in an accelerated world. A world where technology has become a relentless taskmaster. A world where longer work-weeks fatigue us, computers have us chained to our desks, and cell phones accompany us everywhere. A world where televisions connect our homes to the outside, a planet raked with violence where recent dramatic events have altered our lives forever. A world that has us begging the questions: What is important? Where is the meaning in our lives? How do we create a deeper connection to ourselves and others? How do we slow our lives down?

We have a choice. In this journey of life, we can continue to stay in chaos, exhausting ourselves and others around us. Or we can make small changes: take a few deep breaths, sit in meditation in the middle of the day, wear a color that makes us happy, enjoy a sound bath in a bird-filled meadow. Changing one thing, one habit, one way of reacting to the world, changes everything around us. Even the smallest of changes can affect our lives in a profoundly positive way.

The 5-Minute Healer: Self-Healing Techniques for Busy People offers an alternative to the chaos, a way to create a greater balance in ourselves in just a few minutes a day. This book is organized in ten chapters. Each chapter represents years of re-search, study, and application trimmed down to offer a simple introduction to various disciplines. All of the chapters are brimming with simple self-healing solutions and daily routines that can help slow down the pace of our lives.

We decided to use the first-person "I" voice throughout the book to keep it simple. In truth, this book is filled with stories from both of our lives as well as the blending of our practices. This collaborative effort combines the two voices of a nationally known healer who has implemented many of these techniques successfully, helping herself and hundreds of clients, and a writer whose longtime yoga practice, studies in sound healing, daily meditations, and other healing practices included in the book have inspired her to share these discoveries with others. We both come to this endeavor with love in our hearts.

The 5-Minute Healer is a gift, a toolbox filled with time-honored techniques woven together to help create a healthier, happier life. You may relate more closely to one topic than to another. We encourage you to further explore the topics you fall in love with along the way. Some exercises will have immediate results. Others will show their effects over time. All of these techniques are safe and user-friendly.

We invite you to join us on the road to self-healing, a road leading to a more joyful tomorrow for us and our world.

Acknowledgments

FROM MARY CAPONE: There are so many great teachers who have lent their voices to make *The 5-Minute Healer* an authentic tool for self-healing. Many appear in the fine works listed in the bibliography. I would especially like to thank Wendy Bramlett for her guidance on the yoga chapter and her daily inspirational yoga instruction; Barbara Ciletti for her unending advice and unwavering encouragement—you are truly my publishing angel; Vicki Dodd for her profound and revolutionary teachings in the field of sound healing; Lucky Royce for her inspired editing; Suzanne Sarto for her exquisite eye for design; and Tim Benko for his beautiful photography throughout the book. Finally, thanks go to my family, whose constant support and unconditional love make my journey a thing of beauty.

FROM JAN RUPP: I wish to acknowledge my appreciation to life for the multitude of amazing and expansive experiences I have had that have opened up my consciousness and taken me into many cultures, cosmologies, and belief systems. I thank the healers and teachers from many traditions who have entered my life and taken me to unbelievable places, and shared experiences and ancient wisdom with me. I would also like to thank some of the dear friends who have passed who were part of my journey: Barbara Rollinson, who for many years was an incredible support, teacher, "sister," and coworker; Mary Lee Lewis, who insisted I learn astrology and was a great cheerleader for me through many years of evolution in my work; Carl Williams for his love and training in bodywork. In conclusion, I wish to thank my family for all of their support, love, and confidence in me.

Chapter 1

Sound
Therapy

Arias for the Aura, Symphonies for the Soul

AFTER CLIMBING TO THE TOP of the Temple of Inscriptions at Palenque, I sat for a moment of reflection absorbing the late afternoon sun. I closed my eyes and wilted in the steam that lifted from the jungle floor below me. Vapors rose from evaporating puddles and mini-lakes created by a torrential rainstorm the night before. The rich smells of the ever-decaying Mexican jungle filled my lungs with an earthy musk. Above all, it was the penetrating sounds of the rain forest nearby that pierced my experience. The forest erupted with the eerie roar of howler monkeys and tiny insects whose song resembled tinkling bells. Multitudes of jungle birds chanted loudly all around me, accompanied by the constant wind that rustled the thick foliage. There was the sound of faint drumming from an Aztec dance group below. Within minutes, my body began to vibrate in harmony with all the sounds around me and I felt renewed, in balance, and connected with the antiquity of this sacred place. This experience of a "sound bath" in nature reawakened me to the power of sound therapy, a concept centuries old.

Riding the Sound Waves

According to a study conducted by the U.S. Environmental Protection Agency, the wail of a baby crying registers at 90–115 decibels, while a jet engine at takeoff is measured at 120–140 decibels. Amazingly similar! A dripping faucet or cycling refrigerator lists at 40–45 decibels while the household vacuum cleaner and nearby traffic hum in the 75–85 decibel range.

Why do the sounds of nature, such as the waves of the ocean or a babbling brook, soothe us, while humming appliances and the sounds of traffic drive us to distraction? Think of our bodies as instruments, oscillating masses that create individual vibrating fields. What happens to our body when we come in contact with another vibrating field?

More than three hundred years ago a Dutch scientist, Christian Huygens, observed that two clocks placed side by side tend to swing together in a matched rhythm. Later, scientists determined this to be true with as many as five clocks, so long as they were approximately the same size. This phenomenon, referred to as *entrainment,* means that whenever two or more fluctuating bodies or objects in the same field are vibrating at *nearly* the same level, they tend to shift their rhythm so that they are vibrating at *exactly* the same level. Anything that vibrates produces a sound, audible or inaudible, and alters its environment by creating cyclical waves. The environment being altered by sounds may be a lake nearby, the air around us, or even our body.

In recent years, Swiss scientist Hans Jenny offered the world visual evidence of the effect sound has on matter. By transmitting audible vibrations into metal plates filled with matter such as iron filings, moss powders, and liquids, Jenny photographed and filmed shapes formed by sounds from simple to complex. For example, when transmitted into a plate of iron filings, the vowel sound "Oh" formed a perfect circle. Even more interesting, the Sanskrit mantra "OM" produced not only a circle but a complex pattern within the circle consisting of concentric diamonds and triangles. The shape that emerged is nearly identical to the Tantric Buddhist mandala, representing the sacred vibration of creation. Jenny and other scientists concluded that sound has a profound effect on all matter, including the cells and tissues of the human body.

An example of sound and its influence on physical objects occurred at a sound workshop that I conducted. At the beginning of the workshop, I lit a candle to set a relaxing mood. After a whole day of using sound techniques such as chanting, toning, and listening to tapes and musical instruments, I blew out the candle and discovered that a beautiful flower pattern had entrained in the wax. To this day, I keep the candle in my office as a reminder of the power of the sounds around us.

How Does Sound Affect the Human Body?

The human ear is usually credited as the major pathway of sound processing. However, *selective hearing*, or the hearing that takes place between the inner ear and the brain, represents only one way we process sound. *Conductive hearing* involves the entire body. When we come in contact with a sound, the air vibrates around us, penetrating our skin, tissue, especially our bones. In fact, all the cells in our bodies have vibratory properties and therefore are capable of being sound receptors. Our bodies—*our instruments*—literally become *in tune* with the vibrating fields around us.

A good example of harmonious entrainment occurs when a mother breast-feeds her child. In a short time, their heartbeats and breathing synchronize. Studies have shown that entrainment begins even earlier than previously thought. In the womb, the unborn child learns of the world by listening to the mother's breathing, abdomen and uterus sounds, conversations, and especially her heartbeat. The unconscious memory of the maternal heartbeat is most likely the reason why babies are almost always consoled by being held close to a loved one's chest. Our external mother, *Mother Earth*, vibrates at exactly the same level, one megahertz, as that of a healthy human body. In other words, the music of the human body resonates with the music of the earth. No wonder that whenever we are immersed in the powerful vibratory field of nature, it makes us feel more relaxed. It helps retune us.

Unfortunately, the modern world is filled with inharmonious sounds, fields that vibrate at an unhealthy level for our bodies. This ever-increasing assault on our ears, minds, and bodies adds to the stress load, constantly keeping us *out of tune*. Sounds in our homes, such as humming refrigerators, buzzing alarm clocks, beeping microwaves, and the ubiquitous television, invade our day. The buzz of computers, fluorescent lights, insistent beeping intercoms, and ringing phones pollute our office life. Nearby traffic, construction, and airplanes overhead continually accost us. Even when the vibration is below our conscious awareness, the mind continues to process it. In our sleep state, our body is still absorbing the sounds around us.

In addition, each of us radiates a vibrational frequency that reflects our thoughts and emotions. Throughout our lives, sound records our stories, history, and interpretations of all that occurs, creating "audible prints." Recent evidence indicates that the ligand-receptor system, responsible for the chemistry of the mind, is distributed not only to the brain but to the entire body. Thoughts and memories actually exist as molecules of information. These molecules or "audible prints" record in our limbic system, nervous system, tissue, and cellular structure. Patterns of sound get embedded and entrained in the neural pathways that often keep us repeating the same behavior pattern. When we become mindful of the sound of our bodies, we can start to alter our thoughts and emotions.

Sound Therapy: How Does It Work?

Since ancient times, many cultures, including the Greeks, Hebrews, Persians, Romans, and indigenous peoples around the globe, developed and used music therapy for healing illness. Sacred chants appear in the oral history of indigenous tribes dating back centuries. Creation myths of different cultures, including the Maya, often speak of the world being sung into existence. Pythagoras held that sound, especially music, was a potent healing tool. By 1500 B.C., the civilization of India had perfected an intricate system of music called Gandharva, designed to promote healing and to create balance in people's everyday lives.

In more recent years, the Western medical community has investigated the field of sound therapy. Evidence shows that music, after entering the ear, is transformed into impulses that travel the auditory nerve pathways to the thalamus. The thalamus, in turn, stimulates both the hypothalamus, which governs our metabolism, and the limbic system, responsible for hormone secretion. A study conducted at a New York hospital found that stressed patients with elevated blood pressure attained a normalized systolic blood pressure after listening to classical music for just 2.9 minutes and nature sounds for just 3.0 minutes. Other studies have shown that pain medication can be reduced by up to 30 percent with a prescribed music program. Prescriptions for patients in pain at a Kaiser Permanente Medical Center in Los Angeles include periods of soothing music and guided meditations, in some cases eliminating the use of traditional pharmaceuticals altogether. A Yale University study cited music therapy as an effective tool for reaching patients with autism. Another scientific experiment examined the effect sound had on human cells, offering some astounding results. After a short exposure to various sounds, including the human voice singing scales, healthy cells improved oxygen metabolism while unhealthy cells became unstable and even began to disintegrate.

As a result, more and more hospitals are recognizing sound therapy as a valid tool for healing. In many facilities, music is used to enable stroke victims to talk, to reduce ulcer pain, and to decelerate the loss of motor skills in Parkinson's patients. At some facilities, high-pitch ultrasound has been used to dissolve gallstones. Sound therapy has been found to aid in rehabilitation, lower patient anxiety and stress, and even improve the lives of persons with dementia. Music, as a relaxation device, has become a standard in birthing rooms and physical therapy facilities. Hospice programs use music meditations to help people knit together the story of their lives before their death and to assist the people who are left behind with their grief.

Daily applications of healthy sounds can massage organs, release endorphins, change the hormone levels in the body, reduce daily stress and help release trauma embedded in our tissue. Whether you hum a tune, chirp with birds in your backyard, or take a bath in classical melodies, surround yourself with healthy sounds and turn up the volume.

Exercises with Sound

Washing Away the Day's Worries

Put your favorite classical, natural sounds, or relaxation music on your stereo. Remember, it is the music that you prefer that will be the most effective. Lie down in a comfortable position, supporting your neck and knees with pillows if needed. With two speakers, one at your head and one at your feet, allow the music to wash over you, cleansing away the sound pollution of the outside world, all the junk noise your body has absorbed throughout the day. In other words, take a *sound bath*. Breathe deeply, exhale, and release the remaining tension in your body. Feel how the sounds of different instruments penetrate different parts of your body. Add your own voice. Softly hum, sigh, or sing and release the day's frustrations.

While absorbed in your sound bath, notice the areas where pains or aches may develop. This is a signal for you, pointing out where energy is blocked. Many times you can relieve the aches by imagining a flow of energy, a river of water or light running through the painful area. Remember to breathe through it. You may experience an emotional release. Let it wash away with the music.

Now, take it one step further. Stay immersed in the music and allow your imagination to travel to beautiful inner places. Let the music paint a picture. Remember Walt Disney's *Fantasia* and the dancing paintbrushes? Once your picture is finished, allow your five senses to experience it. Let yourself be totally saturated in your surroundings. Notice the sights, smells, tastes, textures, and above all the beauty of this sound-filled world.

The Nature of It

If the opportunity presents itself, go outside for a sound bath in nature. Find a secluded place away from the hustle of the modern world near a stream, waterfall, windy canyon, bird-filled forest, or the ocean. Sit quietly on a blanket on the earth or use a rock or tree stump as your seat. Close your eyes and concentrate on slow, even breathing. After you settle in, exhale and release all the thoughts of the day. Relax and listen to the sounds around you. Remember, the vibration of the earth is the same as that of healthy human tissue. Notice how your mind and body synchronize with these sounds of nature.

The White Noise Treatment

I had a neighbor who kept a fan in her bedroom, even in the middle of winter. When I asked her about it she said, "I only run that at night. I use it to sleep." That was my first introduction to *white noise*. Since then, I've met people who sleep best to the hum of a vacuum cleaner, voices on the television, or music on the radio. White noise, such as the sound of rain, the ocean, the jungle, forests, waterfalls, thunderstorms, birds chirping, even electrical appliances, helps shut out outside disturbances that may be unhealthy to the body.

If your budget allows, purchase tapes of nature sounds at a nearby music store or metaphysical bookstore. Most discount and appliance stores carry white noise devices with a selection of prerecorded soothing sounds at a reasonable price. You can even record your own. Sounds of children laughing, early-morning bird songs, or the rushing of a stream are free for the capture on tape. Let this natural music play in your bedroom and sleep to it, especially if you live near a busy street or in a noisy neighborhood. Pop a tape of indigenous music in your car stereo and block out the sounds of traffic. Try playing Gregorian chants on your house stereo in the morning or eat breakfast to the sounds of the ocean or loon calls on a lake. Play Mozart softly at work on a small cassette player or headphones, if appropriate, to help create a work atmosphere that is both comfortable and relaxing. A small fan may even help block out disturbing outside noise, such as barking dogs or the neighborhood teenagers. Other options are water fountains or a pet canary for a more natural sound. Whatever you choose to use as white noise, you will benefit from creating a harmonious environment that can block out junk noise that invades your day.

A Single Sound

If you're like me, you love singing opera in the shower. Holding a single vowel sound for several scrubs of the bath brush always

leaves me feeling expanded. Picturing myself with the right cos-
tume, something more substantial than what I am wearing, I
imagine myself at Pavarotti's side. I discovered that what I was
actually doing had physical and emotional benefits beyond my
imagining. The process of singing one note for an extended
time can assist in creating chemical and metabolic changes in
the brain, release endorphins, and generally make you feel good.

Singing emphasizes vowels, while talking concentrates on the
consonants. Consonants resonate in the body whereas vowel
sounds wash over the body, soothing all organs with sound. It is
no coincidence that the first vowel sound, "ah," is found in
many ancient religious traditions, such as Christianity's *amen*
and *alleluia*, Muslim's *Allah*, and Hindu's *aum*. This sound sym-
bolizes oneness or unity and is said to open the heart. No wonder it felt so wonderful singing in the church choir as a child.

Below is a list of vowels and the general effect that *toning*,
holding one sound for a period of time, will have on your body.
Try holding each tone through the *exhalation* of several full
breaths, or two to three minutes. Holding a single vowel sound
for this length of time will change brain waves while blending
and reconnecting the exchange between body, mind, and emotions. The hypothalamus, known by medical researchers as the
"brain's brain," is directly affected by this simple act.

A—Chest cavity, but also the body as a whole
E—Throat and upper chest and sides
I—Head cavity
O—Chest cavity and abdomen (down to the navel)
U—Pelvis and lower body
M—Relieves sinus congestion and helps with self-awareness
N—Helps to open the inner ear
OM—Joins the spirit with the body (o = spirit, m grounds it
    in the body)

OO—Draws energy into the body

Ahhhh—Relaxes, reduces stress, and lowers blood pressure

Buzzzz—Reenergizes, changes the brain waves, and increases alertness

Heeee—Encourages relaxing sleep

Sssss—Aids the lungs and helps with asthma, colds, flu, and depression (try practicing with your arms raised over your head and your palms facing the ceiling, giving your lungs plenty of room)

Wooo—Helps the kidneys; relieves anxiety, tiredness, and dizziness

Spend time with these sounds at different pitches—high, middle, and low—and notice how these frequencies affect the different areas of the body, mind, and emotions. Try using the palms of your hands while toning to feel the vibrations moving through your body. Put one hand on your forehead and the other on the back of your head or on your throat to feel the higher tones. For the lower tones, try one palm on the forehead and the other on your chest or lower abdomen. Since each of us is a unique instrument, we may experience these sounds differently from day to day. Even varying moods will result in a different resonance in our bodies.

Go ahead and tone to your heart's content. There is no right or wrong way. Your body will enjoy and appreciate your own sound even if your neighbors do not.

The Hum

Indian Ayurvedic medicine teaches that repressed feelings cause stagnation and energy blockages that crystallize in the tissue of the body. The *hum*, a simple exercise that employs our own voice, resonates in the body, creating a reverberation that can help soften and make energy blockages liquid. Our bodies are composed of more than 70 percent fluid, making them powerful conductors of sound. Using our voice, we can employ one of the most powerful tools of holistic healing.

Sit or stand in a comfortable position, making sure that wherever your body touches the earth you are firmly connected. Begin by saying your name out loud, using your speaking voice as if you are introducing yourself to a new person. For example, I begin with the statement: My name is Mary. Keep repeating your name in that same tone over and over again. Roll it over your tongue as if you were gargling the word. Soon your name will become unrecognizable, blending into a single sound. Mary, Mary, Mary, Mary, Marrrie, Marr, Marrrrr, Rrrrrr. Let the gargling sound soften and pull it into your body by closing your lips and turning it into a hum. Sit with the hum for a moment or two and feel the vibrational quality it has in your body. If you lose the sound of the hum, say your name over again to pick up the thread. Using your own name and voice creates a powerfully unique vibration for your body that nurtures and calms the nervous system. This hum practiced for a minute or two a day can offer profound results. By releasing repressed emotions with this valuable technique, we can become more present in our lives.

To the Beat of Your Own Drum

This sound therapy exercise is borrowed from indigenous peoples worldwide. Using a drum, one of the oldest instruments on the earth, as the sole instrument, shamans and patients alike have been lulled into a trance or altered state of consciousness. Laboratory research has shown that the act of drumming and its sound actually shift the central nervous system. The rhythmic vibrations affect the electrical activities in several motor and sensory areas of the brain. In fact, the continuous beat of a drum contains many sound frequencies that send impulses down more than one nerve pathway, which can literally engage the entire brain. The drumbeat serves as a focusing point for the brain and sensory organs. Even pain can then be filtered out.

In a study involving severely burned babies, the sound of a heartbeat recorded in utero, similar to a drumbeat, was used in place of anesthesia. This sound was effective enough to induce sleep even during painful dressing changes. In Native American cultures, drumming is said to represent the heartbeat of Mother Earth.

Pick up a drum. Flat-headed, round-frame drums or two-headed skin drums are great for deep tones. If you don't have an Indian drum, try an African drum, a snare drum played with brushes, or any type that creates a rich, full tone. Using a drumstick (you can make one out of a dowel with a sock tied to the end with a piece of leather), begin beating the drum softly and steadily with slow monotonous strokes. Continue beating the drum for three to twenty minutes. Research has shown that it will take that much time for your brain waves to switch from beta waves, the conscious eye-opened state, to alpha and theta waves, associated with creativity and a state of ecstasy. Literally beat until your heart is content. It can only help you unwind and free the mind to expand and ponder.

Life is full of music—the laughter of children, the whispering wind through the trees, the songs of birds, and the sound of your own voice. Immerse yourself in healthy sounds each day and create arias for your aura and symphonies for your soul.

Chapter 2

Color
Therapy

Beating the Blues

A FEW YEARS BACK, I found myself in a particularly challenging situation. Along with some dramatic developments on the home front, I was in the midst of changing careers and was broke. One dark, gray morning, I felt my spirits sink somewhere around my ankles. Determined to pull myself up by my bootstraps, I decided to create a new atmosphere in my office by introducing color, the only affordable change I could make. Something had to help. I marched down to a local paint sale with charge card in hand and bought four pails of paint: deep plum, forest green, royal blue, and pale pink. In a single afternoon, I transformed my office with the creative use of these colors on each wall. I felt instantly nourished and at peace. To this day, my spirits are uplifted when I enter the room. This transformation of my mood was so pleasing to me that I was compelled to learn how and why adding color created such a powerful impact. I began an extensive study of color and its healing properties.

The Psychology of Color

- Why is it that Roman Catholic cardinals choose red for their dressing robes?
  It represents spiritual authority.
- What color might you wear while painting a watercolor scene?
  Violet, to inspire creativity.

- Why do business professionals use yellow pads to jot down ideas?

  The color yellow stimulates mental processes and memory.
- What makes blue the perfect color for a comforter for an overactive child?

  It lulls him to sleep.

How can color create moods, invoke feelings, affect impressions, and motivate us into action or repose? Our reaction to color involves both the eye and the nervous system. First, a color enters the eye. The nervous system then sends light signals to the brain. Both the mind and the emotional body respond instantly with likes and dislikes, color preferences that were established in early childhood. A color preference becomes a nonverbal communicator that tells a lot about our personality and self-image. Every aspect of the colors we choose, such as the clothes we wear, the color of our car, and our home interior, communicates something about us. The same is true of our reaction to other people's color choices. The colors others select for their wardrobe and surroundings influence how we feel about that person in subconscious ways.

Colors can motivate us into action or invite us to relax and settle in. A good example of this is well-planned restaurant decor. Fast-food restaurants frequently decorate with red and orange because orange stimulates appetite while red motivates action, prompting us to eat quickly and move on. In contrast, upscale restaurants often use sensual colors such as dusty rose and burgundy, which promote leisurely dining and create a pleasurable experience, inviting us to linger.

Color can aid mental acuity. In one experiment conducted with children with learning disabilities, a yellow transparent film was placed over their reading material. The results indicated that information retention increased markedly when the children's eyes were stimulated by the color yellow.

Other parts of our bodies are also profoundly affected by color. Through various applications, such as clothing, room colors, and light therapy, the color green can reduce blood pressure, red can stimulate circulation, yellow can relieve headaches, blue can reduce swelling, and violet can aid the body in absorbing important minerals.

Think about how we use color when expressing our innermost passions and emotions. In language, color is used to describe not only what we see but also our thoughts and feelings. *She is green with envy. He's yellow. I'm feeling blue. I saw red.* Instantly, we understand what is meant by these statements. It is not the visible color we are expressing, but the enigmatic workings of the human psyche. In effect, we use colors to communicate our emotions because colors have the inherent power to influence the way we feel.

Color penetrates our entire physical and mental well-being. Having the right color on our walls, a rainbow of colors in our wardrobe, the right amount of sunlight, and a variety of hues in our food diet influences the quality of our lives far more than we realize.

Color Therapy and Sunlight

Since the first artist spread pigments on cave walls, people have experimented with the healing value of color. In the ancient world, color was used to activate the emotional, mental, and physical bodies. Five centuries before Christ, Pythagoras used color therapy in his healing practice. Archaeologists in Egypt have discovered an ancient system of color therapy that included chambers of individual colors for curing illnesses. In

Ayurvedic medicine, solarized waters are still used as tonics to reverse imbalances. And indigenous cultures worldwide employ methods like sandpainting to cure illnesses of all types.

Unfortunately, in our modern world, we have all but forgotten the techniques of color therapy for restoring physical and mental health. We have separated ourselves from the natural world and the most powerful source of natural light and color: the sun. We have locked ourselves behind the windows and walls of our homes, offices, classrooms, and automobiles. Even though we may think we are absorbing the beneficial properties of sunlight through our window-filled houses, 98 percent of the natural color spectrum is filtered out.

Science is in the process of rediscovering the benefits of natural sunlight, which contains all the colors of the spectrum. White light, or sunlight, has been found to be extremely effective in treating numerous illnesses, acting as a general tonic for the entire body. It is well-known that the sun helps synthesize vitamin D, assists in the absorption of calcium and other minerals, and stimulates the pituitary gland, the master of the endocrine system. Some scientists believe that exposing all or any part of the body to the sun, *without excess*, will allow the body to naturally extract colors from the spectrum needed to revitalize both health and spirit. A modern prescription for jaundiced babies includes extra fluids and a healthy dose of sunlight. And healthier full-spectrum lighting is now available at local hardware stores to better light our homes and offices.

Conversely, distorted rays of artificial light in our manufactured environments contribute to fatigue, agitate physical behavior, reduce mental clarity, and even promote cell mutations. In a study conducted by the University of California, San Diego, it was concluded that too little sunlight may heighten the risk of ovarian cancer. Results in the study showed that women residing in northern states were eighteen times more likely to die from ovarian cancer than women who resided in sunnier, southern states.

The National Institute of Mental Health reports that over 25 million people experience *winter blues*, depression from a lack of sunlight during the winter months, while an additional 10 million suffer from full-blown seasonal affective disorder, or SAD. Women between the ages of twenty and forty are four times more susceptible to this condition. Scientists believe that the lack of sunlight received by the eye affects our internal biological clock, inducing a hibernation response similar to other mammals. When sunlight hours wane, the body secretes more melatonin, a hormone that regulates sleep, while decreasing the amount of serotonin, a hormone that regulates moods, appetite, and other functions. During the darker months, people with winter depression experience a wide variety of symptoms, including constant fatigue, difficulty concentrating, oversleeping, weight gain due to a change in appetite craving more carbohydrates and sweets, irritability, and depression. There is a growing body of evidence that indicates applying full-spectrum light to the eye decreases the melatonin output while increasing serotonin levels, dramatically reducing depressive symptoms in people who experience the winter blues.

Some color therapists believe that administering specific pure colors with full-spectrum color lamps helps to treat physical ailments and congestion in the body. Patients complaining of insomnia, nervousness, and diarrhea may be treated with various shades of blue. The color green alleviates arthritis pain and also creates a sense of harmony and well-being. Nature, the great healer, is predominantly green. If, however, we cannot find our way to a lush, green meadow, the use of green light can bring peace to our senses.

More and more, the benefits of color are being reintroduced in traditional health-care environments. It was discovered in a hospital trauma ward that a light-filtering green dye painted on a television screen, intended to help relax the eyes of the viewer, stopped the pain of burn victims within a half hour. Using the color green for surgical scrubs has been found to slow down bacterial growth. And, contrary to the original belief that the color white represents sterility and boosts patients' confidence, we now know it has the opposite effect. The "white coat syndrome," a psychological reaction to the stark white of doctors' offices and hospital rooms, can actually produce increased heart rate and blood pressure in many patients. In response to these findings, hospitals across the country are redecorating in dusty plums, pinks, and soft blues in an attempt to create a calmer atmosphere.

Psychotherapists have also used color to facilitate communication between the right and left sides of the brain in order to help their patients become self-aware, confident, and better problem solvers. Being a predominantly left-brained society, we have closed ourselves off to our creative and expansive right brain. To aid in visualizations, some psychotherapists apply color gels to overhead lighting to set the mood and lure their patients into a meditative state. Others decorate their offices to facilitate openness and creativity.

You don't have to wait until you are ready for a sedative to experiment with color in your life. An infusion of color in your everyday environment will restore your health and spirit. Inviting color into your environment can offer surprising results. Take a *color bath* or a *sun splash* to revitalize your weary psyche. Sprinkle your living room with new color accents or set your table in a daring mode. Go to your closet and write a colorful fashion prescription for the day. Drink solarized water to restore your body. Try some of the following simple techniques and immerse yourself in the rainbow.

Exercises with Color

A Sun Splash

Although the sun has recently gotten a bad rap, it is still one of the best sources for restoring color balance and provides nourishment for the earth and our bodies. On the next sunny day, shed as much clothing as prudently possible. With a short-term exposure to sunlight, ten to fifteen minutes before 10:00 A.M. or after 3:00 P.M., the body will naturally extract the colors from the spectrum that it needs. Take a luxurious sunbath during a work break or afternoon errands and enjoy the benefits of the life-giving source of our planet: the sun.

Light It Up

If the weather or the winter season does not permit a siesta under the sun, sit beneath a lamp with a full-spectrum bulb, which simulates the brightness and full spectrum of sunlight. Full-spectrum lighting is now available in many hardware stores, natural product catalogs, and health food stores. Sit beneath a lamp with full-spectrum lighting for five to fifteen minutes in the morning and evening and occasionally glance upward for a few seconds, allowing the light to directly enter your eyes. This simple process helps decrease high melatonin levels, which cause many of our tired and depressive winter symptoms. Although both are effective, research indicates that morning exposure is more effective than evening at chasing away the winter blues. In any case, when the outdoors is off limits, bring the sun inside and light it up.

A Rainbow Bridge

Here's a simple idea that may suggest a return to the sixties. Hang a prism or lead crystal in the window of your bedroom in a position where it will catch the first light of morning. When you wake up, you will be greeted by a full spectrum of color, a virtual rainbow. Breathe in the colors one by one, or allow the entire color spectrum to wash over you. Enjoy the refreshing balance and benefits of the rainbow colors. Try hanging a crystal in your office for an afternoon color bath.

Becoming Your Own Rembrandt

Just as a balanced food diet is needed to maintain a healthy body, providing a full spectrum of color in your visual field is essential in a healthy color diet. Taking in the full spectrum of color through the eye lends nourishment to the body and wards off physical and psychological illnesses. The colors can be subtle or bold and can easily be introduced with simple accents such as throw pillows, area rugs, tablecloths, window coverings, and flower arrangements. You may want to change your accent colors with the season. During cold or rainy seasons, the colors yellow, red, and orange and earth tones encourage physical activity and conserve body warmth. In the warmer months, the tones of green, blue, and violet cool overheated areas and stimulate mental processes. When buying furniture, create a mood with warm colors to stimulate physical ease or cool tones to reduce anxiety.

If you own your home, you may want to experiment with wall and carpet colors. But don't give up if you are a renter. Color accents can be just as revitalizing when they are inexpensive and portable. Remember, it is important to have all the colors of the spectrum within view to create a healthy color diet.

A Palette for Your Palate

The influence of color extends to the food we take into our bodies. The food we eat and the liquid we drink derive their energy and color from the light rays of the sun and the contents of the soil. It's easy to group foods in their proper ray classifications merely by looking at their colors. We do not include foods and beverages that have been dyed with artificial coloring.

A good indication that you are eating a healthy food diet is that within a week you have included the full color spectrum in your food diet: red, orange, yellow, green, blue, purple, and white foods. The following chart offers suggestions for foods within color classifications. Add your own favorite fruits or vegetables to this chart and use it to create a balanced color menu for the week.

Red Foods: tomato, beet, red pepper, radish, red cabbage, berries, red onion, red wine

Orange Foods: cantaloupe, orange carrot, garnet yams, papaya, pumpkin, mango, eggs, squash

Yellow Foods: sweet potato, squash, lemon, yellow pepper, pineapple, banana, yellow onion, corn, parsnip, grapefruit

Green Foods: avocado, asparagus, zucchini, broccoli, pears, green grapes, kiwifruit, cucumber, chives, celery, artichoke, salad, green pepper

Blue Foods: eggplant, blueberries, blue plums, blue cornmeal

Purple Foods: purple plums, purple grapes, blackberries, garlic (remember the pale purple skin), eggplant, broccoli (with its fringed purple top)

White Foods: rice, potato, cauliflower, barley, coconut, white onion, beans: garbanzo, lima, navy

Setting a beautiful table can also add to your visual nourishment. Dress up your table with flowers, colored glasses, pretty plates, napkins, garnishes, and tablecloths. You probably never thought dinner could be this dazzling.

Color Preference

Some psychologists use color testing to analyze their clients' personality traits. Below is a list of colors and what they may indicate about personality. Remember, the colors listed include all shades, values, and tones of that color. For example, a preference for pink, fuchsia, and pinkish peach will be included in the color red. If you lean too much toward one color, you may find your personality traits lying in the imbalance category.

If you prefer *red,* you tend to be energetic, decisive, extroverted, competitive, and impulsive. However, if everything you own is red, you may experience overstimulation and aggressive personality traits.

If you prefer *orange,* you get along well with others, smile easily, and are optimistic and vital. Orange carries a lot of the same wavelengths as yellow. An out-of-balance preference means that you are fickle, shallow, and arrogant.

If *yellow* is your favorite color, you are logical, thorough, courageous, stand up for what you believe in, and are likely to champion causes. You are adaptable, dynamic, and creative. Too much yellow leads to stubborn behavior and being overanalytical.

If you prefer *green*, you are sympathetic, versatile, generous, harmonious, kind, prosperous, and public-minded. An obsessive preference for green can mean you are stubborn, resistant to change, insincere, and dual-natured.

If *blue* is your favorite color, you tend to be relaxed, devoted, artistic, affectionate, and a bit cautious. To the extreme, blue leads to egotistical, lethargic, opinionated, and cold tendencies.

If you prefer *purple*, you are humorous, unique, observant, sensitive, humanitarian, and idealistic. Too much purple leads you to be sarcastic, immature, and self-focused.

Balance is the key to any color preference. Remember, it is important to include all colors in your life to benefit from their harmonious nature.

Color Me Pink

I attended a court case to offer support to a friend who had been ticketed for a traffic violation by an angry officer. As I sat in the courtroom, I concentrated my energy on emitting the color pink, the color of unconditional love. Throughout the proceedings, the judge kept turning his head to look at me. After a radically reduced verdict was reached, the judge smiled widely in my direction.

When you enter a place filled with tension, or are in need of some calm, loving energy in a hurry, imagine the color pink, the color of unconditional love. Take a few deep cleansing breaths and visualize your heart area filling with the color pink. When the feeling of tranquillity permeates your chest, imagine the color extends to your auric field, the energy field around your body. Then picture the color pink being sent farther out, filling the entire area around you. Whether it is your office, house, car, or a baseball stadium, no area is too large to benefit from this harmonious energy. After a few minutes, you'll feel a sense of peace saturate your entire being and the area around you.

The Sun Within

This exercise is great when you are feeling gloomy, pessimistic, or in need of some physical or mental energy. Take a few deep breaths and focus your attention on your solar plexus, the center of your abdomen, just below the sternum. The term *solar* refers to the sun within. Now, visualize the yellow light of the sun expanding in the center of your abdomen. See the sun beams extending from your being in all directions, filling the area you are in. After you spend a few minutes in this lovely sunlight, imagine that this beautiful energy field you have created is filled with the golden light of healing, learning, and love. Bask in this light and enjoy the expansive energy of the sun within.

Solarization of Water

Since our bodies are made up of more than 70 percent water, the influence of the water we drink can never be overstated. Ancient Egyptians perfected a technique to heal and nourish the body by combining drinking water and the powerful rays of the sun. They filled healing bowls with water or the juice of certain fruits or vegetables, then set them in the sun to be charged with the energy of Ra, the sun god. We can use the same principle to solarize water. Solarization is a method that transfers the effect of the color wavelengths and their healing properties to the water itself.

Here's how you do it. Fill a clear glass bottle or pitcher with water and wrap it in a color gel. You can pick up colored gel paper at a photography shop or art supply store. You can also use pure colored glass bottles if they are bright and clear. Place the water in direct sunlight for eight hours. After the water has been solarized, drink a wineglassful every half hour the first day, every hour the second day, and three glassfuls each day thereafter to conclude your treatment. It may taste peppery or metallic due to the energy added to the water.

Using *red* solarized water increases vitality and bodily health by releasing adrenaline into the bloodstream, which increases hemoglobin in the blood and improves circulation.

Orange water influences digestion and builds bodily energy. This water can treat spleen and kidney ailments, bronchitis, and chest conditions. Be careful, though, for too much can lead to overstimulation.

Yellow solarized water is used to cleanse and heal the skin. It can calm the nervous system and has a healing effect on the liver and intestines.

Green water creates a soothing, harmonious effect on blood pressure and heart rate and acts as a tonic for the nerves.

Blue solarized water combats rheumatism, feverish conditions, bleeding, germs, nervousness, and insomnia.

Indigo water is a natural anesthetic and can treat mental disorders, especially obsessions. It is also helpful with diseases of the ears, eyes, and nose.

Violet water restores mental equilibrium and physical coordination. It can be used for the treatment of cerebral diseases, neurosis, rheumatism, and epilepsy. Used at night, it can aid restful sleep.

Drinking solarized water is an easy way to add a splash of color healing to your life.

The Radiant Closet

Over twenty-five years ago, I began a study in color analysis and spent the next five years analyzing clients' skin and eye tones, matching them with the clothing they wore. When my clients wore colors complimentary to their skin, their physical attractiveness was accentuated in remarkable ways. I received a great deal of feedback from my clients about the huge effect this new color information brought to their lives.

Knowing and utilizing the colors that are best for us is a powerful tool. Many of us already know which colors make us look or feel our best. Our closets are filled with them. The following chart offers insight into the physical and psychological effects colors have on us when we wear them. Some general rules: everyone can wear a certain shade, hue, or value of all the colors in the rainbow. Even if a color is not your favorite to wear, you can still include it in your wardrobe as colored underwear or accents to your favorite ensemble.

Color	*Psychological Effects*	*Physical Effects*
Red	Increases self-confidence; improves mental attitude; inspires enthusiasm, vitality, and assertiveness; awakens sensuality.	Increases energy, normalizes heart activity, promotes circulation, helps cold symptoms, neutralizes fatigue, eases asthma symptoms.
Orange	Stimulates creativity and happiness, fosters motivation, promotes mental clarity, balances emotions.	Aids digestion, increases vitality, promotes healthy appetite, eases lower back pain, fortifies blood vessels, soothes joint and connective tissue pain, assists in calcium absorption.
Yellow	Increases memory, reduces anxiety, induces clarity, encourages self-expression and a sense of freedom, inspires happiness and communication with others, cultivates courage.	Increases vitality, relieves headaches, equalizes adrenals, stimulates digestion and elimination, helps with depression.
Green	Encourages self-respect, cultivates efficiency, creates inner harmony.	Balances organ and nervous system functions, supports weight loss, relaxes the eyes, creates physical balance, lowers blood pressure, calms gastrointestinal symptoms, promotes rest and relaxation.

Color	Psychological Effects	Physical Effects
Blue	Encourages creativity, promotes speaking the truth, calms emotional oversensitivity, aids self-awareness, insulates against emotional exhaustion, encourages devotion and inspiration, increases contentment.	Calms overactive thyroid, cools the body, lowers blood pressure, awakens the sense of taste, calms hyperactivity, reduces edema, offers an overall soothing effect.
Purple	Encourages humility and humor, inspires idealism and devotion, assists visualizations, promotes perceptiveness, offers psychic protection.	Balances bodily processes, eases headaches, protects against alcohol overindulgence, promotes mineral assimilation, decreases sensitivity to pain.
Earth tones: Brown and beige	Promotes groundedness, supports mental resilience, offers protective camouflage, aids emotional security.	Assists in balancing hormones in women, supports weight loss and physical strength, fosters a connection to the earth.
Neutral tones: White	Aids in spiritual growth, promotes uplifting and expansive thinking, fosters a sense of purity.	Soothes muscular pain, supports healing, relieves rashes and insect bites.
Black	Inspires receptivity, depth, and mystery; promotes self-control; fosters self-motivation and protection; aids anonymity.	Promotes rest, increases physical balance, assists glandular functions.
Gray	Increases harmony and peacefulness, reduces stress, aids in protection.	Strengthens physical fragility, promotes relaxation.

Source: Mella, Dorothee L. *Color Power.* NM: Domel Artbooks, 1981.

Feel like you're coming down with a cold? Wear a red shirt. Want to feel happy all day? Choose a yellow ensemble. On a diet? Wear brown pants to assist in taking off the pounds. Whatever color you choose to wear, remember that it affects you and people around you. So before opening your closet, write a color prescription for the day and experience the benefits of dressing brilliantly.

Take a sunbath instead of a coffee break. Scramble your wardrobe and dress fearlessly. Fill your home with the colors of the rainbow. Wake up to a prism of light. Bring color into your life and beat the blues every time.

Chapter 3

Aromatherapy

Only Your Nose Knows

EVERY TIME I PASS the windows of the Italian market in North Beach, San Francisco, I am transported by the pungent aromas of hanging balls of Parmesan cheese, prosciutto, and garlic that ride the airwaves like a California surfer. In my mind, I travel the miles and years back to my New York childhood and Sunday dinners filled with boisterous relatives. My stomach rumbles with the sweet and spicy memory of mountainous platters of spaghetti and meatballs, prosciutto and melon, and love. Curious how memories, emotions, and desires can be held in aromas and scents, I followed my nose and discovered the healing world of aromatherapy.

How Are Fragrances Able to Move Us?

Remember the little lace pillows filled with lavender that your grandma used to help her fall asleep? Or how Great-Aunt Martha floated eucalyptus leaves in a steaming bowl of water to create a natural vaporizer for her head colds? Have you ever heard of tucking an infant in bed with a T-shirt sprinkled with breast milk? It never fails to lure the infant to sleep. Somehow in these days of Alka Seltzer, Nyquil, and Sominex, we have lost touch with the old home remedies that require a walk in the woods instead of a walk through the supermarket. For nearly two generations, our society has sadly overlooked the healing power of our sense of smell. Recently, however, the power of aromatherapy has made a penetrating comeback.

Mainstream media has picked up the scent. A *Redbook* article included a list of essential oils with aromas like rosemary and cinnamon that help restore vitality, boost memory, and generally promote healing. The television show *Dateline* presented a segment in which the aromas of peppermint and banana were reported to be scents that aid those who are trying to lose weight. An exposure to the fragrance of popcorn or strawberries makes us exercise harder. And the smell of baking cinnamon buns works as an aphrodisiac for men.

Neurology researchers have found that the scent of green apples helps reduce stress in anxiety patients, making it one of Mother Nature's most powerful tranquilizers. Japanese manufacturers have discovered that releasing the scent of lemon through air ducts in factories increased workers' productivity and mental alertness. Retailers have increased sales by emanating the odor of cookies in their store, while business offices put on the air of professionalism with the scent of high-quality coffee.

It is no mistake that women's perfumes are loaded with floral scents while men's colognes and aftershaves are brimming with woody smells. Perfumeries worldwide know that women are attracted to woody aromas while men are attracted to a floral bouquet. No wonder the scent of rose is synonymous with romance.

Aromatherapies are being introduced in nursing homes as a natural remedy for memory loss, even Alzheimer's disease. The smell of fresh lemon promotes alertness in patients, especially in the morning. Chamomile helps reduce "sun downing," a term used to describe a sense of agitation that occurs in the afternoon. Peppermint lightens the mood while invoking memories connected with food. Lavender fosters social interaction and cinnamon triggers memories, often pleasant, associated with the smell of the spice baking.

Knocked Scentless?

What happens to us when we are deprived of the world of aromas? Have you noticed that when your nose is stuffy, the food you eat somehow loses its flavor? Since our taste buds can only discern four basic flavors—salty, sweet, sour, and bitter—most of what we call the "taste" of food is attributable to our sense of smell, which can discern up to 10,000 aromas. The first step of digestion is actually initiated by the *scent* of our food, which stimulates the production of digestive enzymes. That is why people who have lost their sense of smell have a tendency to be either grossly underweight or overweight. Without the tantalizing aromas of food, people lose their appetite completely or eat continuously, never quite satisfied.

Even NASA learned a lesson about familiar scents. During the first U.S. long-term spaceflight, the astronauts on board experienced olfactory deprivation. They had nothing pleasant to smell except for a lemon-scented towelette for hand cleansing, which became a cherished item. Instead of using the towelettes for washing, they were reserved for special smelling sessions. To avoid this situation in subsequent flights, astronauts were given scented articles. In some cases, familiar smells of home life were reproduced and bottled to help them avoid homesickness.

Ancient Uses

One of the first known uses of healing with fragrances dates back to when people lived in caves and made their beds with aromatic plants that acted as a natural insect repellent. Burning aromatic herbs was one of the earliest recorded treatments for spiritual and physical illnesses. At the time of the pyramids, the art of aromatherapy was general knowledge. When King Tut's tomb was opened, he was found to be surrounded by alabaster urns containing essential oils that, some three thousand years later, still retained their original fragrance.

Natural remedies made from essential oils derived through distillation of plants were used by priests and physicians in Egypt, China, the Middle East, Greece, Rome, and India thousands of years ago. Essential oils were so highly valued by these ancient cultures, they were often equated to the value of gold. One hundred and eighty-eight references to aromatic oils can be found in the Bible. In essence, aromatherapy was one of the first medical treatments practiced by humankind.

Until the 1900s, physicians carried a selection of essential oils in their black bags to be used as regular treatments for illnesses. With the introduction of inorganic chemical drugs, physicians lost touch with these purer, organic counterparts. By the twentieth century, aromatherapy was scarcely known to the modern medical profession. Now, thanks to a swing of the pendulum, people are returning in great numbers to the enormous benefits of these natural medicines.

How Aromas Work Within Us

Essential oils have the ability to directly affect the mind and body. Inhaled, fragrances can stimulate memory, creativity, moods, sexual attraction, and self-healing. And quickly! When aromatic oils are inhaled or applied to the skin, responses have been proven to occur as fast as three seconds. Odor stimuli trigger the limbic or olfactory brain, which is made up of two olfactory bulbs. These bulbs are located at the top and on both sides of the nasal passages and contain up to five million smell receptor cells each. These cells carry scents directly to the limbic system, the governor of memory and emotions, including pain and pleasure. This process then stimulates the release of neuro-transmitters such as endorphins, encephaline, serotonin, and noradrenaline, which can reduce pain, create a sense of euphoria, and relax and energize both mind and body.

During the developmental phases of an embryo, the brain, nervous system, and sense organs are all developed from the cells of the skin. This makes the skin, our largest organ, an excellent vehicle for application. Essential oils applied to the skin, via a bath or massage, reach the internal organs through lymphatic and connective tissues and the circulatory system, triggering a response in the olfactory brain, which regulates our sexuality, likes and dislikes, memory, moods, creativity, and autonomic nervous system.

In the following section we will explore everyday uses of essential oils as well as plants that live in our own backyards and gardens. We will learn how to apply them, when to use them, and the many benefits they provide. Opening our senses to this extraordinary realm of plant fragrances will immerse us in a rich world of aromas and their magic. This is an invitation to stop and smell the roses along the way.

Applications

The Do's and Don'ts of Essential Oils

- When selecting essential oils, cold-processed, absoluts, or Grade A oils are by far the best. Although they are considerably more expensive, the highest-grade oils hold the maximum therapeutic value. Using heat during the extraction process can chemically alter essential oils. Cold processing retains more of the plant's natural properties.

- Essential oils are extremely strong medicines and need to be treated with respect. These oils are 100 to 1,000 times more potent than the plant from which they are derived. Like other strong medicines, they must be kept away from children.

- Use common sense when choosing oils. If you are allergic to a particular plant or have sensitivities to foods, spices, or perfumes derived from that plant, there is a strong possibility you will have a reaction to the oil of that plant.

- Essential oils should *never* be applied directly to the skin. Mixing a few drops of the essence with a fat-based oil allows for an application that is beneficial without harmful side effects. See "Preparing Massage Oils" below. If you should accidentally spill an essential oil directly on your skin, try neutralizing the area with cold, high-fat milk or granulated sugar.

- Taking essential oil internally is *never advisable* unless you are working with a qualified aromatherapist. Even diluted essential oil can cause internal and external burns. Ingesting pure concentrated oil in high dosages can even be fatal.

- *Essential oils are not for infants.* An infant's sense of smell is seven times greater than an adult's. Applying even diluted oils to the crib, clothing, or near the mother's breast can interfere with the bonding process whereby the baby bonds with the natural scent of the mother's body and milk. Exposing an infant to these powerful oils can even impair his sense of smell.

- When pregnant, use essential oils only under the direction of a qualified aromatherapist.

- After an application of bergamot or any citrus oil via a bath or massage, wait four or five hours before exposing your skin to the sun. These oils are photosensitive and can result in brown patches on the skin. Verbena and elenclampine also have extreme photosensitive properties.
- Scented candles are not a good substitute for high-quality essential oils, since they are often infused with synthetic scents that can be mildly toxic and can cause allergic reactions. An aromatherapy shop may have a selection of candles made with pure essences, although you may find them expensive for the amount of time they last; whereas a bottle of essential oil can last for years.

Preparing Massage Oils

Before applying essential oils directly to the skin, *you must first mix them with a carrier oil. Always dilute these powerful oils before applying.* Add three to five drops of essential oil to two tablespoons of a base oil to prepare a special fragrant mixture. A few drops of essential oils added to an unsaturated vegetable oil dilute the essence to eliminate burning side effects while adding elasticity and nutrients to the applied area. Massage the mixture on your body and enjoy the fragrance all day long. Remember, the skin, our largest organ, is an excellent vehicle for application, reaching the body's other organs through connective and lymphatic tissues and the circulatory system.

A good base oil choice is cold-pressed canola oil. Canola oil carries little scent of its own and is compatible with the human body. It is readily available and can be found in your local grocery store. Remember, cold-pressed is the best, since heat processing can extract some of an oil's beneficial properties.

Cold-pressed jojoba oil is another excellent base oil. It is great for the skin, has no scent, and never turns rancid. It is especially good for treating inflamed areas of the skin, such as eczema and psoriasis, and makes a great base for any massage oil used on the face.

Sweet almond oil, with its exceptional penetrating properties, is particularly good for dry or sensitive skin. Unfortunately, it spoils more quickly than other base oils and needs to be refrigerated.

An aromatherapist recently shared with me that fractionated coconut oil is the ultimate carrier oil. It's clean, refined, chemically stable, and similar to our own body fat. Unfortunately, it is not readily available in this country except in large quantities. Perhaps if enough people request this product from their local health food stores we will soon see it on the shelves.

Whatever base oil you choose, mix a garden of fragrances and enjoy the bouquet!

Bathing with Essences

Taking baths with essential oils is an accessible and comforting way to find solace in today's frenzied world. According to anthropologists, the human body evolved in tropical climates. The warm temperature of bathwater can restore an equilibrium that relaxes us at a cellular level. Once a week, give up your hurried shower to enjoy a bath with a fragrant scent. Add three to five drops of your favorite oil to a hot bath and swirl the water thoroughly with your hand to mix it. For an invigorating bath, try adding three to five drops of rosemary or mint to the water. Or combine a few drops of lavender with rosemary for a bath that is both relaxing and refreshing. For a sensuous bath, add a few drops of clary sage, sandalwood, neroli, or jasmine. Add one and a half cups of sea salt and a few drops of eucalyptus to your bath when you have a cold and soak for ten to twenty minutes to help detox and boost the immune system. Find the appropriate oil from the chart at the end of this chapter and add it to your next bath, creating a healing experience.

Aroma Lamps and Other Diffusers

Aroma lamps can transform your home into a garden of fragrances. Add five to ten drops of an essential oil to the water and heat it, dispersing fragrant vapors into the air. These and more expensive electronic diffusers can be purchased at most health food stores, gift shops, and aromatherapy shops. Try using orange, lavender, or pine to create a soothing home environment. The scent of lavender increases alpha-wave production in the brain, the wave activity associated with the state of relaxation. At work, heat up lemon, juniper, or mint to help battle mental fatigue. Rose, lavender, or neroli can blanket your bedroom in a mist of tranquillity. Whatever mood you want to set, aroma lamps are a great way to create it.

An enamel pot of water with a few drops of oil placed on a wood-burning stove or heat vent can also be used to release aromatic vapors in the air. Eucalyptus or citrus oil added to a humidifier's mist creates a disinfectant for a sick person's room. Place three to five drops of oil in the water. Pay careful attention that the water doesn't overheat and destroy the beneficial properties of the oil.

Inhalation, Facial Steams, and Compresses

Prepare an inhalation treatment, especially good for colds, sinus infections, and bronchitis, with a hot (not boiling), steamy bowl of water and three to five drops of essential oil. Essential oils such as eucalyptus, peppermint, and tea tree are excellent for colds and infections. With potent oils such as thyme and ylang-ylang, one or two drops may be sufficient.

This method is also great for facial steams to clean pores and tone the skin. Prepare the steamy mixture and place a towel over your head, bending over the bowl and breathing in the steam for five minutes. Anyone with broken capillaries should use this method with caution, holding the steaming bowl sixteen to eighteen inches away from the face to prevent further ruptures. Asthma sufferers *should not* use this treatment, however, because the steam may aggravate symptoms. A facial steam of lavender is great for all skin types, deodorizing, balancing, and detoxifying the skin. The essence of rose is magnificent for exceptionally dry and inflamed skin types. A sandalwood steam helps relieve acne and inflamed and itching skin, and chamomile cools sunburned skin. In any case, treat yourself to a facial steam and feel as though you've just returned from the salon.

Use a similar preparation technique for hot compresses. Compresses can be used for earaches, stomach cramps, or muscle soreness. Fill a bowl with about a pint of hot water and add two to six drops of your chosen oil. Immerse a natural fabric cloth such as cotton or wool into the aromatherapy mixture. After it is saturated, remove it and wring out the excess water. When your compress is ready, lay it directly on your skin in the affected area. The heat from the compress helps open the pores of the skin, allowing the essential oils to penetrate. A hot compress of eucalyptus can help break up chest congestion. Using a peppermint compress helps relieve headaches and vomiting. A rose compress is a great facial treatment, and orange blossom and lavender compresses can encourage peaceful sleep.

Spicing Up Your Kitchen and Backyard Magic

The kitchen is synonymous with fragrances. Here are a few ways to enjoy beneficial aromas direct from your garden, grocery store, or flower shop. From your spice cupboard create a cinnamon stick–and–clove potpourri to restore vitality. Throw in a star anise to help you feel motivated. Peel a fresh lemon or orange and enjoy the tantalizing smell of the skin and fruit before eating. Throw the peels into a pot of hot water and add some cloves to create a joyful atmosphere. Pick a bouquet of herbs from your garden, such as parsley, basil, lavender, chives, and spearmint. Break off the ends of their leaves beneath your nose and enjoy an aromatic pick-me-up. Peel some gingerroot; smell and taste it to enjoy a warming tonic. Or add fresh-grated gingerroot to your bathwater to help invigorate tired muscles. Gather flowers from your garden or a local florist and enjoy the intoxicating bouquet. Bake a green apple pie, allowing the scent to travel and create a happy and tranquil household.

If you are lucky enough to have lavender growing in your backyard, you already have the ingredients for a lovely bath. Pick a cupful of the scented flowers. Pluck the petals and tie the bundle in a linen napkin or piece of cheesecloth. Put the lavender bag in a ceramic bowl and add boiling water to make a tea for the bath. Wait five minutes. Now draw a bath with the lavender bag tied to the faucet under the running water. Add the tea to the bathwater and bathe in tranquillity and bliss.

Essential Oils and Their Uses

When the doldrums have you, check the following chart for your physical or emotional symptoms and enjoy the restorative powers of essential oils. Apply these oils safely to alleviate your symptoms in a pleasant, uplifting way that heals your body and calms your emotions. Make sure you are familiar with the do's and don'ts of using these powerful oils (given in an earlier section) before beginning. Enjoy!

Essential Oil	Physical Uses	Emotional Uses	Applications
Basil	Asthma, bronchitis, insomnia, colds, nausea, migraines, antiseptic, nervine, gastrointestinal problems, menstrual cramps, spastic muscles, imbalanced hormones	Mental fatigue, antidepressant, grief	Massage, bath, compress, inhalation. Avoid taking in any form during pregnancy. This oil may cause minor irritation when applied to sensitive skin.
Cedar	Acne, skin diseases, hair loss, bronchitis, urinary tract infections	Nervousness, aggression, irritability, dependency, fearfulness	Bath, compress, inhalation, facial steam. Avoid taking in any form during pregnancy.
Chamomile	Inflammation, colitis, fever, headaches, skin problems, flatulence	Sleeplessness, depression, irritability	Bath, massage, inhalation, compress, facial steam
Clary sage*	Menstrual disorders, hypertension, kidney disorders, throat infections, postpartum depression, digestive problems, intestinal and stomach cramping	Depression, PMS, anger, midlife crisis, paranoia, nervousness, grief, negativity	Bath, inhalation, compress, aroma lamp
Clove	Diarrhea, intestinal disorders, respiratory illness, antispasmodic	Memory loss, vulnerability, fear	Aroma lamp, inhalation, humidifier. Avoid taking in any form during pregnancy. This oil may cause minor irritation when applied to sensitive skin.

Eucalyptus	Measles, herpes, asthma, bronchitis, throat and sinus infections, kidney infections, fever, acne, muscle aches	Mental fatigue, emotional stress, inability to focus	Bath, massage, inhalation, aroma lamp, humidifier
Jasmine*	Joint stiffness, muscle spasms, frigidity, impotence, uterine disorders	Pessimism, anxiety, low self-esteem, fearfulness, paranoia, negativity	Bath, massage, inhalation, aroma lamp
Juniper	Acne, bladder infections, sluggish kidneys, sore muscles, detoxify blood	Negativity, anxiety, ungroundedness	Bath, massage, inhalation, aroma lamp
Lavender**	Abscesses, burns, migraines, motion sickness, asthma, bronchitis, tissue healing, bites and stings, rheumatism, hypertension, immune deficiencies (persistent infections)	Sleeplessness, hysteria, nervousness, moodiness, depression, stress, irritability	Bath, massage, facial steam, inhalation, aroma lamp, compress
Lemon	Infections of all kinds, head colds, sinusitis, sore throat, inflammation in the mouth, warts, herpes, fevers, varicose veins, fragile capillaries, hypertension, nose bleeds, hemorrhages, acidic conditions	Mental confusion, being overly emotional, depression	Bath, massage, inhalation, aroma lamp, compress. Do not use this oil prior to sunbathing or direct sun exposure due to its photosensitive properties.
Lemongrass	Fluid retention, lymphatic congestion, kidney disorders, bladder infections, varicose veins, weak digestion, oily skin	Inability to concentrate, morning moodiness, fatigue	Aroma lamp, inhalation, facial steam, humidifier. This oil may cause minor irritation when applied to sensitive skin.

Essential Oil	Physical Uses	Emotional Uses	Applications
Orange	Kidney and bladder disorders, gingivitis, fevers, colds, constipation, heart spasms, irregular heartbeat	Apprehension, grief, loneliness, nervousness, self-consciousness	Bath, massage, aroma lamp, inhalation. Do not use this oil prior to sunbathing or direct sun exposure due to its photosensitive properties.
Peppermint	Colds, indigestion, migraines, stomach pain, vertigo, vomiting, neuralgia, asthma, heart palpitations, headaches, flatulence, fainting, liver disorders, sinus congestion, fainting, insect bites	Fatigue, exhaustion, forgetfulness, inability to focus	Aroma lamp, inhalation, compress, humidifier
Rose*	Constipation, irregular menstruation and uterine disorders, skin problems, shingles, sterility, herpes simplex, liver congestion, headaches, frigidity, conjunctivitis	Sadness, grief, depression, disappointment	Bath, massage, inhalation, facial steam, aroma lamp, compress
Rosemary	Arteriosclerosis, arthritis, scalp disinfectant, headaches, nervous exhaustion, diarrhea, high cholesterol, hypertension, gallstones, gout	Insecurity, fearfulness, nervousness, memory loss, mental fatigue	Bath, massage, inhalation, compress

Sandalwood*	Male genital problems, urinary afflictions, nausea, vomiting, diarrhea, cardiovascular disorders, cystitis, tuberculosis, throat infections, strep infection, staph infection, sciatica, lumbago, acne, dry skin, itching	Self-centeredness, loneliness, aggression, nervousness, negativity	Bath, massage, inhalation, compress, aroma lamp, humidifier, facial steam
Sweet marjoram	Antispasmodic, migraines, insomnia, rheumatism, constipation	Agitation, sadness, grief, sleeplessness, nervousness, exhaustion	Bath, massage, inhalation, aroma lamp, compress. Avoid taking in any form during pregnancy.
Tea tree	Fungus, virus, immune deficiencies, ringworm, athlete's foot, lice, cold sores, mouth ulcers, respiratory infections, skin infections, insect bites, cuts, body ulcers	Depression, lack of clarity	Bath, massage, inhalation, compress
Vetiver	Muscle tension, anorexia, aging skin, insomnia	Postpartum depression, stress, ungroundedness, nervous anxiety	Bath, massage, inhalation, facial steam
Ylang-ylang*	Heart palpitations, hypertension, tachycardia, impotence, frigidity, skin regulator, cell regenerator, hair loss	Sleeplessness, nervous tension, anger, frustration, depression, negativity	Bath, massage, inhalation, facial steam, aroma lamp

*Clary sage, jasmine, rose, sandalwood, and ylang-ylang are euphoric oils and can help with the grief of a loved one's passing.
**Lavendin, a hybrid of lavender, is cheaper and more pungent but lacks the medicinal qualities of pure lavender.

Take a facial steam with the essence of rose. Bathe in the soothing aroma of lavender. Fill an aroma lamp with the essence of
pine and turn your home into a gentle forest. Rub mint leaves
between your fingers and delight in a "scentsational" pick-me-
up. Whichever way you choose, follow your nose to the world
of aromatherapy and enjoy healing for your body and tranquillity for your soul.

Chapter 4

Breathing
Techniques

Portable Prana

I SPENT AN EVENING as a guest speaker addressing a trans-personal psychology class at a local college. Thanks to my hurried speaking and shallow breathing, I delivered the equivalent of a six-week course in a single evening. After the lecture, students came up to me to thank me for my efforts. Although they may have appreciated my power-packed speech, my body did not. Light-headed and exhausted, I made it to my car just as my body gave out. Events like that make me increasingly aware of the stress in my system due to inappropriate breathing. Today, before addressing audiences, as I look out over a sea of smiling faces I take a few deep, cleansing breaths and, with renewed energy and clarity, I begin.

Every Breath You Take

It has always fascinated me that the human body can go for weeks without food and for days without sleep or water. Yet life will cease to exist within minutes without air. Our primary source of sustenance is derived from the air around us. In other words, life *is* breath. In yoga, the breath is called *prana*, meaning "life force." Since we carry it with us everywhere, I like to call it "portable *prana*." The more life force, or *prana*, we take into our bodies, the more alive we become.

Every cell in our body is reliant on our oxygen-rich exchange with the natural world around us. On inhalation, we derive oxygen from the air via our respiratory system. When oxygen enters the bloodstream, it attaches to the hemoglobin of the red blood cell, which transports it throughout the body. When cells receive this oxygen, they exchange it for an equal amount of carbon dioxide, a gaseous waste. The carbon dioxide is then returned to the lungs and expelled through our exhalation. Deep inhalation stimulates healthy blood circulation, the primary nurturer of the brain and body. Sound exhalation rids the body of toxicity. We exchange over 3,000 gallons of air with the natural world each day.

Most of us, however, have a habit of shallow breathing or hyperventilating, taking more air in than we let out, allowing the breath to reach only the upper lungs. This breathing pattern promotes a carbon dioxide buildup in the body, resulting in dizziness, headaches, muscle tension, fatigue, and a general sense of anxiety. Without proper oxygenation our cells die or function at a declined level. Normally, when we exhale we squeeze breath from only the middle and top of our lungs, leaving the lower lungs filled with unreleased stagnant air. Although our lungs have the capacity to hold five liters of air, by hyperventilating we take in only three liters, constantly leaving a liter or more of stale air in the lungs. This stagnant air allows bacilli to build up, weakening the lung tissue and leaving it open to infection.

Medical research has shown that tuberculosis, heart disease, asthma, and digestive and blood pressure disorders may be caused in large part by poor breathing techniques. A study conducted in a New York hospital found that deep breathing lowered elevated systolic pressure to normal levels in 2.7 minutes. Another study examined respiration as a powerful governor of heart rate variability. Unconsciously holding the breath or engaging in shallow breathing can result in the constriction of blood vessels and rapid heart rate, which increases blood pressure by making the heart work harder. Abnormal breathing and an accelerated heart rate are often an early sign of autonomic dysfunction in a number of diseases.

Our breathing pattern directly affects the way we think and feel. Improper breathing deprives the brain (an organ that requires three times the air supply of our other organs) of the oxygen it needs to function properly. In addition, our lungs contain a high concentration of peptides, proteins involved in emotions and thoughts. When the brain is deprived of a healthy level of oxygen, thinking becomes unclear. Brain cells die every four minutes without proper oxygenation. Unconscious rapid breathing, often associated with stress and anxiety, turns on the nervous system's "fight or flight" response, resulting in fearfulness and poor concentration while releasing stress hormones that can wear down the body at an accelerated rate. Many psychotherapists now believe that anxiety may, in fact, be *caused* by improper breathing. Hyperventilation can magnify emotional conflicts and psychological distress, causing a person to react to a situation with heightened nervousness and fear.

Emotional and physical traumas can form holding patterns in our breath, often beginning at infancy when a baby entrains with her mother's breathing patterns (see Chapter 1). This idea of trauma and holding our breath is even embedded in our language: "It took my breath away," "I held my breath," "It knocked the breath out of me." Trauma that has happened long ago may still be waiting for us to fully exhale.

Even corporate America is recognizing the power of proper breathing as a motivation tool for employees. By offering deep-breathing training seminars, some companies have found that this simple solution can increase mental alertness, stamina, and physical flexibility, positively impacting productivity and health care expenditures.

Becoming a Better Breather

If you think you have escaped the category of hyperventilators, try counting the number of breaths you take per minute. If you are breathing an average of twelve to fifteen times per minute, you fall into this category. (Six to eight breaths per minute is considered best for body-mind health.) This pattern, coupled with shallow chest breathing, indicating insufficient exhalation, wins you the "bad breathing award."

Although breathing is an unconscious function, just like the beating of our heart and the workings of our digestive systems and other bodily functions, we can take control of it whenever we desire. Great power lies in the choice to become conscious of our breath. Conscious breathing allows us to feel the inward and outward flow of life. Proper oxygenation quiets the body's nervous system, relaxes tensions, and brings about a sense of peace that permeates our thoughts and emotions. Deep breathing stimulates the hypothalamus and a parasympathetic response in the body, decreasing muscle tension, heart rate, and blood pressure. Slowing the breath to a rate of six breaths per minute synchronizes it with cardiovascular rhythms that also have a six-per-minute cycle. Increased blood circulation due to deep breathing enhances liver function, improves digestion, and nourishes the brain. Sound exhalation leaves room for fresh air to enter the lungs and ventilate the entire body, giving our heart time to rest, reducing the risk of heart attack, and lowering our blood pressure. With our body no longer starving for air, healthy tissue is restored to our lungs, making it easier to fight off infectious diseases. Whenever we choose to be conscious of our breath, we become cocreators of our life force.

In our hectic lives, it's easy for us to take breathing for granted. This oxygen-rich exchange with nature is one of life's most overlooked gifts. By taking a few minutes out of each day to experience our breath, we can become aware of the powerful tool we carry with us everywhere we go. The simple techniques I've included in this chapter can travel with you to the office, to your home, or accompany you wherever you go. Try this: the next time you feel your body tense while waiting in yet another line, take a few deep breaths and enjoy the benefits of their calming energy. Breath is a precious gift to all of us. It is absolutely free and contains zero calories—so partake fully.

Exercises with Breath

One Breath at a Time

Here's a simple technique that can help you become a better "belly breather."

This yoga practice of *pranayama*, or "Complete Breath," is believed to have the power to awaken the body's own healing energy. But don't let that scare you. It's a simple exercise that works to distribute the breath evenly throughout the entire lung, while inhaling and exhaling fully. Five to fifteen minutes of *pranayama* a day offers great benefits, restoring high levels of mental clarity and bodily health.

Sit with your spine erect. Or, if space allows, lie down in a comfortable position, with your legs outstretched or bent at the knees. With one hand on your chest and the other on your abdomen, exhale fully until you feel your lungs are emptied. Pause for a moment and enjoy the stillness. Take a deep, slow breath through your nose, filling your lower lungs and feeling your belly rise and expand. Continue inhaling, filling your mid-lungs and expanding your ribs and then filling your upper lungs until you feel your chest rise. Draw your shoulders up slightly and fill the highest part of the lungs. Pause and experience the expansiveness of your full lungs. Then exhale through your nose, first feeling your shoulders lower and your chest withdraw as your breath leaves your upper lungs, then feeling your ribs contract as you exhale from your mid-lungs, and finally allowing your abdomen to deflate. Breathe in again deeply, rounding your belly first, then filling your chest. Relax and continue until your breath has reached an even rhythm of six to eight deep breaths per minute. Enjoy this act of being a conscious breather and feel the synchronicity of your breath with the breath of the universe.

Taking a Breather

One of the simplest exercises we can do to become a better breather is to take a breathing holiday. Often, especially during the winter months, we stay locked indoors in our homes and offices, even our cars, breathing stale recycled air over and over again. Remember, the lungs love moist, fresh, oxygen-filled air. With a little effort, we can give the lungs a mini-holiday, every day.

Take a few minutes a day to go outdoors and breathe in. Instead of parking your car inside your garage at home or at the office, try parking outside and fill your lungs with crisp refreshing air on the walk to the front door. The air outdoors typically contains more negative ions than recycled air, with summer air richer in negative ions than winter air. Negative ions are beneficial for optimum health. If you live in a city that has poor air quality, plan breathing vacations to areas with cleaner air that is filled with negative ions, such as the mountains, ocean, lakes, rivers, and parks loaded with plants and trees. Take a five-minute stroll along a nature-filled walking trail. Many cities are now seeing the wisdom of maintaining open-space trails. A trip to a botanical garden over your lunch hour can be a revitalizing adventure. Your lungs will love the warm, moist atmosphere as you exchange your CO_2 with the oxygen-rich green world of nature.

"Breathe" Cards

Inspired by the business card of a breathing coach, I made a dozen cards that simply have the word "Breathe" written on them. These simple cards always serve as a gentle reminder to take several deep, nurturing breaths before I move on in my day.

Make a dozen business-size cards with the simple command "Breathe" printed on them. Place them around the areas that you frequent each day such as your computer desk, the inside of your office door, your car dashboard, the refrigerator, your nightstand, where you hang your keys. Then when you come across these reminders, take a few deep breaths. I find that just seeing the word "Breathe" makes me automatically take a deep breath. Remember, our unconscious breathing often returns us to shallow breathing patterns. By sprinkling these simple reminders around our environments each day, we can take a moment to become conscious of our breath, feeding the whole body, especially the brain, with the oxygen it needs.

Conscious Breathing

The intake of air produced by deep breathing provides a current of energy that can be channeled anywhere in the body. It can be used to fuel a specific function of the body, to relieve muscular or physical pain, or to soothe a tired mind. The key to this exercise is to remain focused, consciously waiting until your body chooses the next inhalation. The point of this exercise is not to hold your breath until you are ready to pass out but to become aware of the natural rhythm of your breathing. Letting your mind wander can allow you to slip back into an unconscious breathing pattern.

Begin with the Complete Breath, or *pranayama*, described above, breathing deeply and slowly through your nose and this time exhaling through your mouth. At the end of your exhalation, consciously wait … retaining your breath for a count of ten or until your body chooses to inhale. Continue this process and let the time between breaths be a period for your whole body to release tension, storing fuel for later use.

Now breathe and locate specific areas in your body that have remained tense or are still in pain. Invite your energizing breath to those particular areas. Exhale consciously, letting the tension go. Relax deeply during the pause between breaths. Continue for several minutes.

Tree of Life

This technique is one I use to release tension. It can be done whenever you have several minutes of uninterrupted time. You may choose to lie down, sit, or stand for this exercise.

Begin by breathing deeply in through your nose and exhaling through your open mouth. After several complete breaths, close your eyes. Imagine that you are being transformed into a magnificent tree. The breath you take comes up through your roots deep within the earth, entering the soles of your feet. Breathe in slowly, steadily, as if you are pulling the air up through your feet, ankles, legs, torso, to the upper chest. Then release the breath by blowing out through your open mouth. Continue this for several breaths.

Now, with your next inhalation, imagine as you pull the breath from the soles of your feet—*your roots*—upward, you are brushing away all of the tension stored in your body. Release this tension with your exhalation, by blowing it out through your open mouth. Feel the movement of the air blowing away tension and outmoded patterns, just as the autumn winds blow the leaves from the limbs of a tree. Visualize the tension willingly leaving your body just as the autumn leaves offer themselves to the wind. Continue for several more breaths.

Now imagine that, as these worn, stagnant energies are released from your body into the air, they burst into leaves of bright colors sparkling in the sunlight, making room for new growth. Continue your cleansing breath, sweeping up the tension and releasing it into the air. Imagine the shower of bright leaves leaving your body with each exhale. Continue for several breaths, noticing all the sensations you are experiencing.

Tense Up and Relax

This breathing technique can be used to discover where you are holding tension in your body. Take a deep breath and flex your body as tightly as you can. Hold that position for two breaths. Take another deep breath and on the exhalation relax the entire body muscle by muscle. Notice where your tensions lie, areas that are difficult to relax. Direct your next inhalation into these areas and on your exhalation, release.

Now that you are totally relaxed, notice how much tension you carry in your body every day. Make a commitment to fully relax. You can do this breathing exercise stuck in traffic or on a coffee break without too much notice being taken. Better yet, make it an herbal tea break.

Victorious Breath

After you become comfortable with the Complete Breath, or *pranayama*, as described earlier in this chapter, try the "Victorious," or *ujjayi*, breath. The *ujjayi* breath is the yoga *pranayama* technique with the simple addition of sound. With a slight closure at the root of the throat or your epiglottis, you can give voice to your breath. Listening to the sound of your *ujjayi* breath can give you a greater sense of your breathing rhythm and its subtle changes, helping you to understand your breath patterns and how to even the flow of your breath.

Lie down in a comfortable position, with your legs outstretched or bent at the knees. Take several *pranayama* breaths. On your next inhalation, open your mouth and inhale softly, noticing where your breath touches your throat. This is the area you want to *slightly* constrict. Once you find the area, close your mouth and exhale. Your breath will now have a soft but audible tone. Now inhale, continuing to constrict the epiglottis, and notice the sound of your breath. Stay with this breathing for five to fifteen minutes, making the tone of your inhalations and exhalations as even as you can.

The Ocean Breath

In this exercise it is important to follow both the inhalation and the exhalation of your breath. The primary function of this breath is to conduct a two-way relationship with universal energies. With each inhalation, we open up and draw in the living energies of the universe. With each exhalation we yield, expelling personal tensions and outmoded patterns.

For this exercise, imagine that your breath mirrors the ebb and flow of the sea. Begin by paying close attention to your breath. Breathe in. Follow your breath, noticing the sensation of the energy flowing into your body. Notice any area of your body that is resistant or in pain and bring your breath to that part of the body. After several complete breaths, imagine that the moist sea air is filling your lungs and the sound of crashing waves is charging your body with enormous energy. While exhaling, notice the sensation of the energy flow leaving your body. The waves are retreating, flowing back to the sea, along with all of your stresses and unwanted energies. Close your eyes and continue this breathing until you feel in sync with the universe around you.

Alternate Nostril Exercise

Since ancient times, meditators of many beliefs have maintained that the key to successful meditation is proper breath control. Yogis of the Himalayas took this idea one step further.

They believe that it is imperative to use controlled nostril breathing during meditation. During the course of a day, our breath has a natural cycle that alternates between the right and left nostrils, switching dominance every four hours. This mirrors the natural polarity of our brains, body, and mind and helps us to maintain a balance between these polarities. We can simulate nostril breathing and further assist this natural balancing act with the following breathing exercise.

Sit in a cross-legged position on the floor or in a comfortable chair. Hold your left nostril with your thumb, completely closing it off, and breathe in slowly through your right nostril for a count of ten. With your index finger, hold your right nostril closed for a count of four. Release your thumb from your left nostril and exhale for a count of ten. Pause for a count of four. Now breathe in slowly through your left nostril for a count of ten. Close off the left nostril with your thumb. Hold for four counts. Release your index finger and exhale through your right nostril for a count of ten. Continue this rotation for several minutes, always remembering to release your hold and switch nostrils before exhaling. Enjoy as complete balance is restored.

Breathing—we all have to do it. Why not do it consciously and enjoy all that breath has to offer? Relaxation of the body and clarity of the mind are just two of the rewards. It might be just what you need to make it through another hectic day. All you have to do is breathe in, one, two, three ...

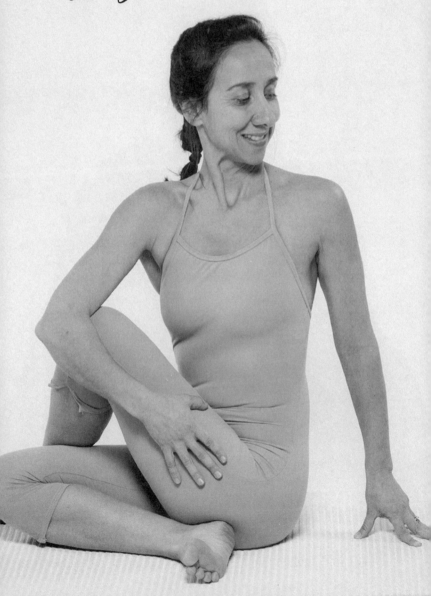

Chapter 5

Yoga

Asanas for Everyone

A YOGA TEACHER once told me, "Life is a dance. Move too fast and you'll soon lose balance and exhaust yourself. If you choose to sit the dance out, rigidity and stiffness become your companions. Dance with grace and fluidity and you'll move through life with the beauty of a swan." Even though I have yet to become a yoga master, yoga is an important part of my daily practice. I have developed a personal program that increases my flexibility and physical strength, balances my emotions, and quiets my chattering mind. Although I may still appear to be an ordinary human being, in my quiet moments I glimpse the reflection of a shimmering wing.

Yoga: What It Can Do for You

What exercise program reduces stress; increases flexibility; tones muscles; improves the endocrine, nervous, and circulatory systems; harmonizes the body-mind connection; and leaves you with a more positive outlook on life? *Yoga.* This six thousand–year–old practice offers the perfect safe and relaxing, no-stress workout. The word *yoga* comes from the Sanskrit word *yogah*, which means "to join or combine." With the combination of deep breathing and proper body alignment, yoga helps both the body and mind learn how to relax. Its calming energy relaxes the mind and stimulates clearer thinking and creativity. This mind-body discipline doesn't stop there. Yoga is a serious program to keep our bodies fit, greatly improving our overall health.

The physical benefits of practicing yoga are numerous. Yoga oxygenates the body's systems, boosting circulation and benefiting the heart. Like other exercise disciplines, yoga aids cardiovascular functions, increasing the body's volume of blood, lowering blood pressure, and taking stress off the heart muscle. With increased blood volume, more oxygen and nutrients are carried to the cells, washing the tissues, massaging internal organs, and removing toxins. Unlike strenuous exercise programs in which this added fuel is consumed during the exercise period, yoga's moderate techniques allow the body to store this energy bonus for later use. Even arteriosclerosis, hardening of the arteries, is aided by this versatile exercise. During the stretching and bending of yoga poses, arteries are elongated, increasing the blood vessels' elasticity while balancing the flow of blood from the heart to all parts of the body.

Through aligned stretching, yoga activates the entire glandular system, balancing its secretions, which regulate digestion, energy levels, growth, immune defenses, and sexual functions. Everyday traumas affect these secretions, creating physical and emotional imbalance. Yoga postures place specific and continued pressure on the various glands, helping to stimulate and restore glandular equilibrium, which in turn calms and balances the emotions. Long-term yoga practice strengthens the entire autoimmune system, the failure of which is responsible for many diseases.

The subtle exercise of yoga relaxes and tones muscles. Throughout the day, many of our muscles remain unused even with a strenuous exercise program. Yoga postures work all the muscles of the body, restoring underused muscles to proper working order. During yoga, postures are attained slowly and held for a specific amount of time, followed by complete relaxation. This process allows the body to completely relax and de-stress in a natural way.

Yoga often succeeds where diets fail. Although this exercise program is not about counting calories, yoga can bring about a body awareness that fosters a healthier approach to eating. Besides leaner muscles and increased strength, yoga practitioners often develop a loving connection to their body, making them more aware of what nutrition the body truly needs. In addition, the inner mindfulness of yoga can offer a place to reflect on emotional issues once buried by food.

Yoga can even help counteract the aging process, giving the body more freedom, increased inner strength, and flexibility of the spine and joints. Children naturally move their spines with perfect fluidity, but by age thirty many people find it impossible to touch their toes without bending their knees. Over time, ligaments tighten and shorten from lack of use and improper posture. Our daily routines add greatly to this condition. Jobs often require us to sit for hours, trapped behind desks, hunched over keyboards or telephone receivers, compressing our spines. Gently stretching stiff and injured joints helps free them of calcium buildup. By stretching ligaments and tendons, yoga frees the energy locked in our spines, restoring fluidity and flexibility to our bodies and melting away the stiffness that is often associated with aging.

The Breath of It

The single most important factor contributing to the potency of yoga is breath. For centuries, Eastern medical traditions have maintained that proper breath is a major component of health. For the most part, Western medicine has ignored this factor. As in other areas, however, awareness on this subject is increasing. Today many recovery programs include deep, conscious breathing, meditation, and yoga to alleviate stress, decrease blood pressure and muscle tension, increase circulation, and strengthen the immune system. For a more complete understanding of the benefits of conscious breathing, refer to Chapter 4.

The Latin word for breath is *spiritus*. Although yoga is neither a religion nor a physical therapy, it combines a little of both. Through deep breathing and stretching, the practice of yoga allows us to explore our personal powers of self-healing and regeneration by stimulating our life force. With conscious breathing, we can experience an expansive feeling beyond the body, one that helps us get in touch with our inner selves, our spirit.

The Do's and Don'ts

- Whether you are choosing one yoga pose or the series of yoga poses presented later in this chapter, wear clothing that is nonrestrictive and comfortable for the room's temperature.
- Practice in a private, peaceful, well-ventilated space, avoiding direct sunlight. Make sure that you can sit comfortably on a nonstick yoga mat or exercise mat reserved just for this purpose. You can purchase an inexpensive yoga mat in a variety of catalogs, yoga magazines, and sporting goods and health food stores. Other accessories you may want to add are a foam block and a cotton or dense wool blanket approximately 60 × 80 inches.
- Always practice in bare feet, without shoes or socks. Bare feet not only keep you from sliding but also directly connect you with the earth.
- It's best not to practice on a full stomach.
- Throughout the session, keep your focus on your breath. Inhale and exhale at a slow, even rate and never hold your

breath. Breath is probably the single most important part of any exercise program, especially yoga. So don't forget to *breathe, breathe, breathe.* Feel what is happening to you as you stretch—the stimulation, the release of energy, and finally the relaxation.

- Remember, never stretch farther than your limit and always listen to the innate knowledge of your body. The word for yoga poses is *asanas,* which means "postures comfortably held." You should never experience muscular pain when attempting a pose or posture. If you are in pain, stop the posture immediately.

If you have never attempted stretching or yoga poses before, you may want to consult a friend who can guide you. Working together with someone can be inspiring and fun. After practicing for a few weeks or months, if you like the way it feels, you can expand your practice by consulting one of the many self-guiding manuals or videos available today. If you are an interactive learner, get thee to a beginning yoga class and enjoy.

Stretching It

Each of the following poses can be done by itself for a couple of minutes a day, producing some very good results. A more desired program, however, would include a twenty- to thirty-minute workout performing all the *asanas* listed below.

You might think it's impossible to fit more activity into your already crowded schedule. Think of it this way: A session of yoga requires less time than it takes to watch a TV sitcom. Americans spend 40 percent of their free time, or an average of fifteen to eighteen hours a week, in front of the television. When was the last time your television helped restore your mental and physical health?

Try these ideas: Take half of your lunch hour and transform your office into a sanctuary. Wake up a half hour earlier in the morning and greet the day with renewed peace of mind. If you have young kids at home, add a yoga session to your daily routine. Your children will enjoy learning some of the postures along with you, such as Child's Pose and Lion's Pose. Or, try substituting your more strenuous workout with yoga two or three times a week. It was recently discovered that strenuous workouts release endorphins in the bloodstream but not in the brain. So although your body may feel better after an advanced aerobics class or weightlifting session, frequently your mind remains as stressed and unhappy as when you started. Yoga releases endorphins to both the brain and the bloodstream, relaxing both the body and mind.

Everyone can learn to achieve simple yoga postures regardless of flexibility or age by beginning slowly and gently. It is not necessary to be in top physical condition or to devote a lot of time to learning about these practices to benefit from them. Still, the practice of yoga is not a miracle cure. It is estimated to take one month of yoga for every year you have experienced a painful condition before you notice results. Start now and enjoy *asanas* for everyone.

Yoga Postures

1. Complete Breath (Pranayama)

Whether I am wiping the sleep from my eyes or returning home after a long day, I begin my yoga session with the Complete Breath (*pranayama*). Although you may already be familiar with the Complete Breath from Chapter 4, this valuable technique is worth repeating. *Pranayama* is a simple exercise that works to distribute the breath evenly throughout the entire lung, while inhaling and exhaling fully. It is proclaimed by the *yogis* to activate the body's own healing power. Beginning your session with *pranayama* helps to integrate the breath into the entire practice.

Lie down in a comfortable position, with your legs out-stretched or bent at the knees. (See Figure 1.) With one hand on your chest and the other on your abdomen, empty your lungs with a long breath, exhaling slowly through the nose. Pause for a moment and enjoy the stillness. By concentrating on keeping the breath slow and even, your lungs will naturally empty and refill at an appropriate rate. Take a deep, slow breath through your nose, filling your lower lungs, feeling your belly rise and expand. Continue inhaling, filling your mid-lungs and expanding your ribs and then filling your upper lungs until you feel your chest rise. Draw your shoulders up slightly, filling the highest part of the lungs. Pause and experience the expansive-ness of your full lungs. Then exhale through your nose, first feeling your shoulders lower and your chest withdraw as your breath leaves your upper lungs, then feeling your ribs contract as you exhale from your mid-lungs, and finally allowing your abdomen to deflate. Notice the natural pause your body takes after this complete exhalation. Breathe in again deeply, round-

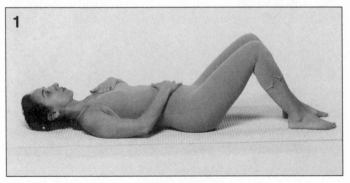

Complete Breath

ing your belly first, then filling your chest. Repeat this process five times or until your breath slows to six to ten deep breaths per minute. When you feel more comfortable in this pose, try extending the pause between your inhalations and exhalations. This posture increases circulation, reduces toxins, regulates blood pressure, relaxes the heart, and improves digestion. Enjoy the flow of life-giving *prana*.

2. Fun Roll

Sit comfortably on the floor and pull your knees to your chest. Embracing your legs with both arms, relax your neck and drop your head to your knees. (See Figure 2A.) Now, gently roll back on your spine and rock back and forth like a human sphere. (See Figure 2B.) Remember to take slow inhalations through your nose, exhaling fully. Feel the stretch in your vertebrae and the gentle massage your spine is experiencing. After a minute or eight to ten rolls, gradually come to a stop. Stretch your limbs and lie flat on your back with your arms at your sides. This exercise stretches and energizes the spinal column.

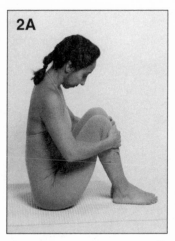

Fun Roll

3. Bellows Pose (Bhastrika'sana)

Lie on your back with your legs straight out and take several deep breaths before beginning. Now engage your outstretched legs by extending through your heels. Inhale and pull your right leg up to your chest and hold it firmly with both hands, keeping your left leg straight and engaged. (See Figure 3A.) Hold for eight to ten seconds and then, exhaling, release your leg slowly, lowering it to the floor. Now, bring your left leg up to your chest and hold for eight to ten seconds. Release on the exhalation and lower your leg to the floor. Next, pull both legs to your chest, enveloping both legs firmly in your arms. (See Figure 3B.) Hold for eight to ten seconds and with your exhalation release slowly, lowering your legs to the floor in unison. Repeat the entire process three times. You may feel a slight pull in your groin area. Stretch only to a comfortable position. This pose activates the lower adrenal glands, removes stomach gas, and relieves high blood pressure, stomach upset, and constipation.

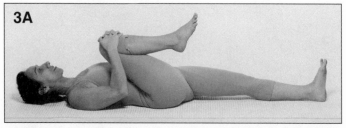

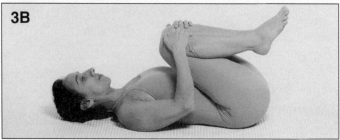

Bellows Pose

4. Knee and Thigh Stretch (Badrasana)

From a seated position, sitting squarely on your "sit bones," bend your knees and slowly draw your feet toward your perineum until the soles of your feet rest flat against each other. (See Figure 4A.) Add a bolster, block, or rolled-up blanket under each knee if this stretch is too intense. Before continuing, make sure that the base of your pelvis is balanced, neither tucked under nor extended forward. You may use a pillow or mat under your buttocks to elevate slightly to help you sit correctly. Clasp your ankles with your hands and gradually release your knees toward the floor. (See Figure 4B.) Breathe deeply into your pelvis and lower abdominal region. Visualize the tension draining from your entire perineal area. Hold for a count of ten. Now, releasing your knees, allow them to return to the unstretched position without coming out of the pose. Repeat three times. This posture releases tension stored in the pelvis and hip area.

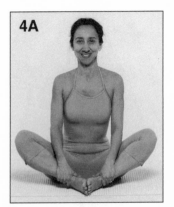 

Knee and Thigh Stretch

5. The Spinal Twist (Ardha Matsyendrasana)

In yoga, it is widely believed that a yielding mind and unyielding spine can seldom be found together. If our body is tied in knots, frequently our thoughts and emotions are, too. Are you tied into knots over a dilemma? Are you twisting your thoughts about a problem before you? Do you always need to be in control and therefore become inflexible? Here's a pose that can help get you untwisted. Imagining yourself as a king cobra allows you to twist effortlessly to view another direction. With this posture you have made a decision to turn, see life from a new angle, unwind from old rigidities. Although this pose may seem complicated at first, it is easy to get the hang of and can provide wonderful relief for spinal tensions and pressures.

Begin this pose seated on your mat, both legs extended outward. Fold your right leg back until your right heel is against your left thigh. Then place your left foot in front of your right shin, resting the sole of your foot on the floor. (See Figure 5A.) Place your left hand on the floor directly behind you. Grasp your left knee or thigh with your right hand. Now you are ready for the twist. Slowly turn the trunk of your body as far left as comfortably possible, tucking your chin to your chest and turning your head last to look over your left shoulder. (See Figure 5B.) This stretch comes from the deep waist and should not be forced by the head rotation or leveraging too much from the hand placement on the knee. Remember to stretch only as far as your comfort zone allows. Make sure your spine is straight, your chin close to your shoulder. Hold for a count of thirty. *Don't forget to breathe.* Repeat to the right side.

If you feel comfortable with this position, continue with it twice more to each side. For a more challenging pose, begin with your legs outstretched before you. Fold your right leg back until your right heel is against your left thigh. Then take hold of your left ankle and swing it over your right knee, resting the sole of your foot on the floor. Place your left hand on the floor directly behind you. Grasp your left knee or thigh with your right hand.

Then follow the same instructions for twisting. (See Figure 5C.)
Remember to stretch only as far as your comfort zone allows.

Repeat the Spinal Twist for a total of three times on each
side. This pose will become easier as you practice more. If you

cannot do the more advanced
twist, return to the modified
version. Both offer great benefits for your spine. Never do
this pose if you are pregnant,
trying to get pregnant, or
menstruating. This posture
reduces constipation and jaun-
dice, helps correct an enlarged
liver and spleen, strengthens
back muscles, and releases
tension in the neck.

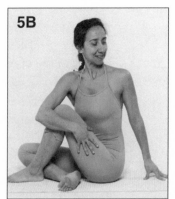

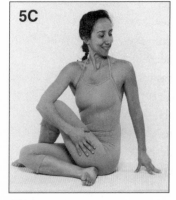

The Spinal Twist

6. The Cat/Cow Posture

Start on all fours with your knees hip distance apart. Support
the weight of your torso and your spine with the firm planting
of your hands and feet. (See Figure 6A.) In the first part of this

posture you will imitate a relaxed cow. On the inhalation, drop your pelvis, allowing your stomach to sag between your knees by pressing down with your shins and raising your tailbone. Slowly raise your head upward, feeling your spine and belly fully relax like a full-bellied cow. (See Figure 6B.) On exhalation, drop your tailbone between your legs, hollowing out the belly. Curl your head downward and back toward your tail-

bone. Press into the floor and broaden your back by raising your spine one vertebra at a time until it is arched like an aroused cat. (See Figure 6C.) Repeat this stretch eight times, dropping your pelvis and raising your head on each inhalation and lowering your head and arching your back on each exhalation. This posture tones the abdomen, back, and legs; releases neck and shoulder tension; and relieves constipation and gas.

The Cat/Cow Posture

7. Modified Downward-Facing Dog
(Adho Mukha Svanasana)

Using a chair to perform this traditional pose puts less stress on the wrists and shoulders while still offering a great spinal stretch. Begin by standing with your feet about two feet apart, facing a folding chair or one of traditional height placed a couple of feet in front of you. Bending up and over the waist, by hollowing out the belly and pulling up from the center, bring your palms to the chair in front of you. Now adjust your pose by walking your feet back until you feel your arms and spine extending together in one line. Keep your arm bones high to avoid collapsing into the shoulders. Now, pull up and back from the belly, adjusting most of your weight onto your legs. Allow your neck to relax as you feel the full stretch in your spine. (See Figure 7.) If your hamstrings are tight in this pose, give a slight bend in the knees to avoid overstretching your lower back. Rest in this posture for several cleansing breaths. This posture stretches the entire spine, strengthens the legs and arms, and releases tension in the pelvis and spine.

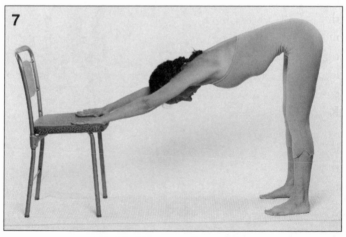

Modified Downward-Facing Dog

8. Standing Forward Bend (Uttanasana)

This posture should be performed very slowly for maximum benefit. Begin standing with your feet parallel, placed hip distance apart, and your arms resting at your sides. Give yourself a gentle bend in the knee to help keep you from overextending your hamstrings and back. Take a deep breath. Raise your arms overhead and place your palms together. (See Figure 8A.) Exhaling, drop your head forward by simply relaxing the muscles in your neck and bend up and over the waist by hollowing out the belly. With your arms extended, continue bending forward as if you were performing a swan dive. Gradually release the entire spinal column by allowing the front of your body to drop forward in a hanging position. Deepen the bend in your knees until your feel that the tension in your back is released. As the stretch moves into your hips, lift your buttocks toward the ceiling, gently stretching your hamstrings. Keeping your belly lifting, roll your weight to the balls of your feet and your toes. Continue to allow your head, neck, arms, and shoulders to hang freely and, if possible, place your hands on the floor in front of you. (See Figure 8B.) Rest for thirty seconds. To come out of this pose, reverse the movement, starting with the hips. Roll up slowly, one vertebra at a time, feeling the entire spine. When you are standing again, lean backward slightly with arms extended over your head to counterbalance the forward stretch and hold for ten seconds. Repeat three times.

For a more challenging stretch repeat this pose with your legs straight, first coming to your fingertips (see Figure 8C) and then resting in a full forward bend. (See Figure 8D.) If this is too intense on the hamstrings, return to the bent knee version. Repeat this *asana* a total of three times. This posture gives rest to the heart, increases blood supply to the head, and releases the entire back side of the body.

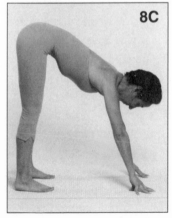

Standing Forward Bend

9. *Side Angle Pose* (Utthita Parshvakonasana)

Stand with a wide stance between your feet with your front foot facing forward and your back foot planted at a forty-five-degree angle. Raise your arms to shoulder height, extending them out to the side. Now bend your front leg at an angle, ninety degrees or less if this is too intense, keeping in line with the forward foot. (See Figure 9A.) Inhale. Keep engaging the legs, especially the back foot, and elongate from your torso as

you extend over your forward knee. Lower your elbow onto your bent knee, keeping the weight of your elbow light. Align the front and back body over the forward knee until they are open equally. On the next in breath, extend your other arm overhead. (See Figure 9B.) Adjust the pose until you feel a comfortable stretch between the little toe side of the back foot and the pinkie finger of the extended arm. Hold for several breaths. Repeat twice on each side. This posture opens the side body while strengthening the body's core.

Side Angle Pose

10. Triangle Pose (Trikonasana)

The Triangle Pose is a strengthening pose designed to increase balance and poise. In this posture, we become like a triangle—steady, balanced, strong, and viewing life clearly from a different angle.

Stand with a wide stance between your feet with your right foot in front facing forward and your left foot in back planted at a forty-five-degree angle. As you shift into the pose, continue

Triangle Pose

engaging your back leg, pressing the little toe side of your back foot into the mat. Raise your arms to shoulder level. (See Figure 10A.) Breathe in deeply and, on your exhalation, bend gracefully over your right leg, extending your torso from the pelvis to the crown of your head. With your left arm to your waist, place your right hand anywhere from your shin to your ankle. Now adjust your pose by making sure that your torso is directly over your forward leg and that both the front and the back body are open equally. Keeping your knees straight (be careful not to hyperextend them), extend your left arm as far as you comfortably can. (See Figure 10B.) If this is too uncomfortable, place your hand back on your waist. Feel the stretch in your left side. Hold for several breaths. Slowly rise to a standing position. Repeat this stretch to your left. Continue stretching until you have completed this pose three times on each side. To assist in finding an open front and back body, try placing your hand on a block. (See Figure 10C.) This posture balances appetite, strengthens and aligns the legs, releases tension in the torso, and relaxes trunk muscles.

11. The Cobra Pose (Bhujangasana)

There are very few animals more feared than the cobra. A bite from its powerful jaws means instant death. Yet the snake is able to shed its skin in renewal and in many cultures represents fertility and wisdom. As we extend in the Cobra Pose we are embracing the attributes of the cobra, the power of renewal, and the recognition of the poisons of depression or negative thought in our lives. Like the snake, we too can wisely glide through life waiting for the right moment to ascend.

Lie face-down on your mat with your forehead resting on the floor, allowing all your muscles to relax. Draw your legs together and engage them by pressing them gently into the floor. Place your elbows beneath your shoulders and, with your forearms resting on your mat, place your hands flat on the floor with your fingers pointing forward. Inhale deeply. On your exhalation, elongate your torso by slowly lifting with your arms until you are propped on your elbows and forearms, raising your head and chest, eyes looking forward. (See Figure 11A.) Your spine will have a gentle curve. Continue pressing your legs gently into the floor and enjoy the extension from head to toe. Hold for thirty seconds. To release, slowly and gently lower your chest first, and then your head, to the original floor position. Repeat three times.

For a more advanced pose, place your hands flat on the floor beneath your shoulders with your fingers pointing forward and your elbows drawn close to your body. Inhale deeply. On your exhalation, elongate your torso by slowly ex-

The Cobra Pose

tending your arms, raising your head and chest, and rocking your spine back and forth until you have reached a full, even arc with your eyes looking upward. (See Figure 11B.) Keep your elbows close to your ribs and relax your buttocks. Only stretch within your comfort zone, paying close attention so that there is no uncomfortable tension in your lower back. If there is, lower down to a more comfortable level. Hold for several breaths. To release, slowly and gently lower your chest first, and then your head, to the original floor position. If this is too difficult on your spine, hips, or lower back, return to the modified position of propping yourself up on your elbows. Repeat this entire exercise three times. The Cobra Pose strengthens the spine, improves flexibility, exercises cranial nerves, and readjusts the spinal column.

12. Child's Pose (Balasana)

Whether countering a backbend, such as the Cobra Pose, or for a simple restorative posture, try the Child's Pose. Childlike in its simplicity, this *asana* offers a way to completely relax and let go.

Begin by sitting on your heels with your feet together and knees slightly apart. Ground your thighs onto your shins and your shins into the floor. (See Figure 12A.) Drop your "sit bones" into your heels by curling your tailbone under as you extend over your folded legs, allowing gravity to take your torso until your forehead rests on the floor in front of you. (See Figure 12B.) You can rest your arms beside you or, for an additional stretch, reach your hands out as far as you can on the floor before you, fully stretching your trunk and spine. (See Figure 12C.) Remember to keep your tailbone tucked with the weight falling back toward your heels. Relax for several breaths in this comfortable position. The Child's Pose strengthens stomach muscles, helps regulate the menstrual cycle, and offers deep relaxation.

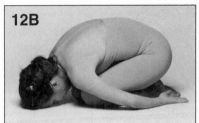

Child's Pose

13. The Lion's Pose (Simbhasana)

The Lion's Pose is designed to help us recognize the lion within and to give it voice. It is intended to lift the muscles in the face and neck and with added sound helps release the pent-up stresses of the day. Through the ages the lion has been used as a symbol of power, glory, magnificence, strength, ferocity, and knowledge. By performing this posture, you are saluting those attributes within you, a lion in all its glory. Remember that it is impossible to be truly gentle if you are suppressing the lion within.

Begin by sitting on your heels with your hands resting on your knees. (See Figure 13A.) On the inhalation feel a lift in your chest until you feel a full but gentle arch in your spine. Now you are a lion ready to roar. Spread your fingers as far as possible like the claws of a lion. With your jaws open wide, stretch your tongue out toward your chin and open your eyes wide. (See Figure 13B.) You should feel a firm pull on all of the muscles in your face and neck. If not, intensify your facial posture. When you reach the extreme position, forcefully exhale with your throat open and let out a roar. Don't worry what you sound or look like. Allow your roar to clear your throat of unreleased words and emotions. Return to a relaxed position. Repeat this posture three times. If you have difficulty sitting on your knees, add a folded blanket between your buttocks and heels and place your hands on your thighs. After you are finished, rest back in the Child's Pose. The Lion's Pose relaxes facial and throat tension and releases the neck muscles.

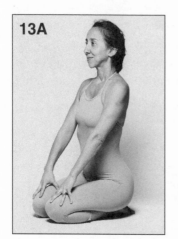 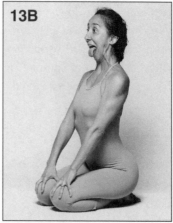

The Lion's Pose

14. The Corpse Pose (Shvanasana)

The Corpse Pose offers complete relaxation. As human beings we use an incredible amount of energy resisting life's encounters and challenges. In this pose, we emanate the silence of death, wherein lie great possibilities for peace and powerful rebirth. This posture is an important finishing touch for any yoga practice because it allows the body to incorporate the information and sensations the *asanas* have provided.

To begin this posture, lie comfortably on your back with your legs outstretched or bent at the knee, arms at your sides, palms up, and your mind alert. (See Figure 14.) Closing your eyes, breathe deeply and quietly for several minutes without moving a muscle, allowing your body to drop down toward the floor, melding with the earth. First notice your legs ground toward the earth, then your arms, your torso, and so on, until you are completely relaxed and one with the earth. Now, on your next inhalation, draw in the bright golden light of *prana* through your nostrils, allowing it to expand into your lungs and head, then traveling down your chest cavity, pelvis, and legs and finally down and out your fingertips and toes. Feel your body tingle with energy and total relaxation. After five minutes or whenever you are ready, return to the living world. This posture offers complete relaxation of the body and mind, lowers blood pressure, and relaxes the heart.

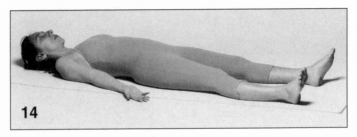

The Corpse Pose

Feeling jittery? Take a few complete breaths and calm your body and mind. Having emotional or physical problems? Relax into a posture and enjoy all that yoga has to offer. Yoga, with its perfect combination of stretching and breathing, can add grace, poise, and relaxation to all your daily activities. Whether you are rising from sleep or taking a break at your desk, stretch your body out and move with the beauty of a swan.

Chapter 6

The Mind

Blueprints for a Better You

IT TOOK THE BIRTH of my child to inspire me to create a re-birth in my own life. With my first child, I was determined not to make the same mistakes that haunted me from my early past. I became my idea of a perfect mother, sacrificing all of my own wants and needs to benefit my family. I continued to run a full-time business with very little day care and I always wore a smile. At home, I cooked and cared for my family with the utmost urgency. Exhausted, I found myself going through the motions mechanically without the natural joy that parent-hood can provide. It took a stay in the hospital before I realized I was blindly repeating patterns and habits that were handed to me in my childhood—habits that were imprinted deeply on my subconscious mind. My need for perfection and over-achievement reared its ugly head, cutting me off from spon-taneity and joy. I understood then that to become a healthy parent to my child required me to unlock the doors of my sub-conscious mind and reclaim my world on my own terms. It was time to look back.

Stress: An American Epidemic?

Each year, eleven million Americans are stricken with stress-induced depression. Nine out of ten Americans claim that they undergo high levels of stress at least once a week, and one out of four say they live with disabling stress every day. In California, in the 1980s alone, worker's compensation claims due to mental stress rose 700 percent. Tranquilizers and anti-anxiety and anti-depressant medications account for over 40 percent of written prescriptions in the United States each year, while over 60 percent of doctor's visits are due to stress-related illnesses. It's no surprise that stress is cited as the number one killer of Americans. One out of seven American men suffer from heart disease before sixty. Two out of five adults have hypertension. Insomnia, chronic fatigue, and other stress-related, crippling diseases have become as familiar as the common cold. We are a society under siege.

What is at the core of this stress? How can we respond to all these demands in a healthier way? In this chapter, we will explore the roles of the nervous system and the emotions and learn ways to reconstruct the mysterious governor called the mind.

The Illusive Mind

The dictionary defines the mind as the element of the self that feels, wills, perceives, thinks, and reasons, and as the seat of consciousness of memory and remembrance. The mind is often divided into the conscious, subconscious, unconscious, and superconscious, or higher self.

Woven into our culture and language are sayings like "Mind over matter," "I changed my mind," "It blows my mind," "In my mind's eye." These simple expressions illustrate the various interpretations of the mind and the power it has in our lives. But where is the mind exactly? Often we think of the mind as residing in the brain. We now know that this is only partially true. In the 1970s, a famous neurosurgeon concluded, after three decades of recording findings from thousands of neurosurgeries and brain probes, that the mind could not be located solely in the brain but in the energy field, the aura, that surrounded the body. Many scientists now agree with ancient teachings that the mind or consciousness is processed by the brain but not produced by it. Recent evidence indicates that the ligand-receptor system, responsible for the chemistry of the mind, is distributed not only to the brain but to the entire body. Thoughts and memories actually exist in the body as molecules of information. This evidence suggests that the mind is in the brain, the cells of the body, and the energy field surrounding the body, thus firmly establishing the body-mind connection.

Stress: The Nature of It

Stress is a natural part of life. When dealt with properly, it can become a powerful learning and motivational tool. Left unresolved, however, stressful issues wear down the body. Childhood crises become the roots of many disorders such as adult depression, gastrointestinal diseases, lung and heart disease, and many autoimmune diseases. Sound familiar?

There is much evidence that difficult or tragic experiences alter the neurochemical system. Stress rewires the nerve circuitry, creating in our bodies a sensitivity to stress similar to an allergy. Sensitization lowers our tolerance to stress, producing an overreaction in our bodies and minds. Even the slightest incident will send messages to the brain, causing the same biochemical reaction as if we were in imminent danger, turning on the fight-flight-or-freeze mechanism. Stress that looms ominous in our adult life may be due to destructive subconscious tapes from the past.

This biochemical pounding wears the body down at an accelerated rate, weakening our immune systems, eating away at our digestive systems, and leaving us more vulnerable to cancer and other diseases. The hormones released during stress disable our hearts and lungs, promoting strokes and asthma.

How do we change these destructive patterns? On the surface, our life may seem to be in order. But what feeds our thoughts and actions? How have we incorporated others' judgments into our belief systems and identity? What parts of ourselves have we left behind?

How Does the Subconscious Mind Work?

Think of our subconscious mind as a scribe or tape recorder whose job it is to record information about everything in our environment. Like a tape recorder, it makes no judgment about the contents of the material it takes in. The subconscious mind knows no chronology, logic, or humor. It merely records. Everything we say, think, and hear registers as literal truth. What we are told as a child by our parents, siblings, and society is absorbed as bits of our story that eventually become a part of us.

The subconscious also stores habits and patterns referred to as procedural memory. Riding a bicycle and feeding and dressing ourselves are a few of the habits maintained by the subconscious to assist us in everyday life. Following orders blindly, the subconscious can also maintain destructive and harmful habits and patterns. As children, we may acquire specific fears from our parents and siblings, such as squeamishness about spiders or snakes or fear of the dark. Other patterns, such as worrying, self-doubt, perfectionism, a need to overachieve, or even obsessive cleaning, can, if unchecked, continue to play themselves out in a robotic fashion.

The same subconscious that is responsible for storing information, early messages, and learned patterns also regulates our major body functions. While we are busy living our everyday lives, the subconscious is making sure that our hearts beat, our lungs breathe in and out, and our stomach and intestines digest food. Many of the diseases that manifest in our bodies are connected with the storage of negative thoughts and expressions in the subconscious mind. If there are too many negative tapes stored in the subconscious, the cells of the body undergo constant stress.

Conscious attention needs to be paid to *what we say* as well as our thoughts and feelings, our internal dialogue, our attitudes and recurring imagery. Phrases like "I'll be damned," "I'm sick to death," "Stupid," "I need a break," "It's a pain in the neck," "You're breaking my back" all have the potential to become self-fulfilling prophecies. Remember, the subconscious merely records information and governs bodily functions. If we use the phrase "It makes me sick" over and over again, we may find that our subconscious has cooperated by granting us the illness we have unwittingly focused on. Equally powerful are the thoughts and feelings we suppress, the things we refuse to feel or say. By giving attention to these aspects, we become aware of our part in empowering undesirable situations and occurrences in our lives. Awareness is only part of the total cure. We must replace the old patterns and habits with healthier ones.

With awareness and cooperation between the conscious, subconscious, and higher self, *our soul,* we can choose to change outmoded habits and destructive patterns that block our life force and alter the course of our lives.

The Self, True or False

In our striving to adapt to the world's demands, we develop a *persona*, a mask we hide behind. This masked self emerges while our true, boundless spirit learns to go underground, to protect itself, to lock itself away. After many years of acting out the false self, we forget who we truly are.

This true self that is wounded is waiting to be retrieved, healed, and given a voice in our lives. How do we begin to retrace the steps of time? First, we might ask ourselves these questions: Who have I become? How have I changed and shifted to seek approval from or rebel against parents, society, or peers? What aspects of my true self have I left behind? What were my original dreams?

By addressing these issues and more, we begin to unlock the mysterious workings of our subconscious mind and embark on the journey of self-renewal.

Understanding Trauma

To explore deeper into the mysterious mind, we'll take a look at the nature of trauma. Examining trauma may shed some more light on the complex reaction to stress that many people experience.

Most of us have had experiences that have left us feeling overwhelmed or in a state of shock from which it took us quite some time to recover our sense of safety and healthy boundaries. Some examples are physical abuse, car accidents, serious falls, assaults, and natural disasters. When our nervous systems are totally overwhelmed and immobilized, our reptilian brain takes over with the only perceived option left, the freeze response. Our systems simply shut down, leaving us feeling frozen in time and space. We remain in a state in which our nervous systems have the accelerator and brake on simultaneously. This frozen state creates a loss of connection from self and others, often leaving us feeling isolated.

Trauma has a cumulative effect and, after experiencing a great deal of it, the nervous system begins to perceive many ordinary stimuli as life threatening. Everyday things like the sound of a slamming door or the wail of sirens can lead to a full-blown panic attack. In the past this was referred to as shell shock and more recently as post-traumatic stress disorder. In older indigenous cultures it is referred to as soul loss.

Luckily, there is a vast body of research that has shed new light on the nature of trauma. Much of this new understanding comes from observations of animals in the wild who, like humans, have a limbic and reptilian brain. The human brain is made up of three parts. The reptilian brain, the oldest portion of the brain, we have in common with reptiles and is associated with survival. The limbic or mammalian brain is the emotional and feeling portion of the brain, and the neocortex, the cognitive brain, makes us unique as humans and is connected to thinking, perceiving, and creativity. When animals come into danger and experience the fight-or-flight response, they release this trapped energy by shaking and trembling. Humans tend to block this response, deeming this natural physiological response as inappropriate behavior.

Although in this chapter we do not address the resolution of trauma, awareness of this condition is important. There are many practitioners available to more fully address these issues, as well as books on the subject, several of which are listed in the bibliography for this chapter.

Phoenix Rising

Why take on our past in the first place? Maybe your life is comfortable the way it is. What's the point of stirring up old memories? Or maybe you have become so attached to the painful past that releasing it may bring with it a loss of identity. The purpose of this chapter is to take a look at the parts of our past that are still causing us pain and disruption, then create a loving environment to work in and begin transforming them.

It is my belief that to heal, we must dig down deep and face what is fueling our thoughts and feelings. By rebuilding our subconscious mind, we can truly heal from the inside out, making the other therapies and techniques examined in this book more effective. Take a few minutes out of your day to examine your foundation and begin reconstructing your subconscious mind for a better you.

Exercises for a Better You

Affirmations for the Here and Now

Creative visualization is a term used to describe the process of our body-mind communication. Thoughts and images form in our mind, consciously and unconsciously. Our mind then sends these messages to our bodies as signals or commands. When we become conscious of this process, we can take control of it, creating our own positive thoughts and images. Through positive affirmations we can supply healthy messages to replace negative or limiting ones.

Affirmations are most easily planted in the subconscious if you say them right before you go to sleep or when you first wake up in the morning. You can say them silently or out loud, or to strengthen your response you can record them and listen to them around the house, in the office, or in your car. Reciting them while in a frenzied mood, however, may give the subconscious conflicting messages. For example, if you snarl, "I am love," in the midst of an attack of rage, the mind may associate rage with love.

Here are a few affirmations that I have found helpful in my life. Feel free to create ones that better fit your own needs. Always use the present tense and positive language. The subconscious will resonate more fully with a positive statement than with one containing a negative. Instead of saying "I am not worthless," say "I am worthy."

- I am the author of my life.
- I am safe.
- I am a vessel for creative energies.
- I have an inner wisdom that guides me.
- My inner light creates miracles in my daily life.
- Love works through me and fills my life.
- I am able to express all my feelings.
- I am a radiant expression of life.
- I unconditionally love and accept my body.
- My body is full of vitality and health.
- My age is ideal and I look forward to each new day.
- I am greatly loved.
- Every moment is a new creation.
- My life is full of infinite possibilities.

Using affirmations can help change the negative messages stored in our subconscious mind, replacing them with happier, healthier ones. Create a list of your own and truly become the author of your own life.

Mirror, Mirror, on the Wall

Here's a quick exercise that has a powerful impact. I have seen miracles happen with the use of this technique. Looking into your eyes in a mirror, say your name, then say something wonderful to yourself such as: *I love everything about me; I am growing and changing; I am happy with who I am; I appreciate myself; The past is behind me; I am beautiful in every way; I accept my feelings as part of myself.* Do this four or five times daily. If you feel resistance, stick with it. Feelings of sadness, self-hatred, or the belief that you are lying to yourself may rise to the surface. Looking in the mirror will reflect the feelings you have about yourself, pointing out areas that need attention. Pay attention to feelings that arise. These observations may lead to a deeper

understanding of the issues that lie beneath. You are not looking for physical evaluation with this exercise. The focus is on
correcting the relationship with the self. Remember, you are re-
programming your subconscious mind. Have patience. It may
take time. One glorious day you will look in the mirror and
know that what you are saying is true!

Laughter, the Best Medicine

I recently came across the statistic that children laugh, on
average, four hundred times a day, compared to an adult, who
averages fifteen laughs a day. *What happened to our joy?* Current scientific research indicates that laughter increases the
amount of oxygen in the bloodstream, helps clear congestion
in the lungs, provides muscle conditioning and pain relief, increases circulation and nutrients to tissues throughout the
body, and helps boost the immune system. Laughter releases
healthy brain hormones that reduce stress; helps us approach
problems from a new, more creative, angle; and even prolongs
life. It can even give your abdominals a workout, massage your
internal organs, and create "happy" cells.

Take a few minutes out of the day to have a good laugh. Try
watching a segment of your favorite funny movie. Put your
feet up and read a silly joke book or a favorite author who tickles
your funny bone. Share stories with your friends or create a
humor circle in which everyone brings funny stories with
laughter as its sole purpose. Take a sound bath with a self-made
or bought laughing tape and roll on the floor with joviality.
Or try this: Invite three or four of your friends over for a children's game of laughter. Each person lies on the floor in a circle
with his or her head on the next person's stomach. One person
begins by releasing the sound "ha" several times, with each person taking a turn until spontaneous laughter erupts. Whenever

things are at their worst, remember to laugh, transforming your stress with a chuckle!

Journaling Your Beliefs

Here are some journal-writing exercises that are as powerful as they are simple. Try exploring the following questions. You might be surprised at what you discover about yourself.

When writing on these topics, there is one simple rule to follow: There *are* no rules. You are writing to discover what your subconscious messages are, not to win the Great American Novel contest. Don't get hung up on the use of proper grammar or sentence structure. Your message can be written using simple phrases or images. Don't stop to edit or rewrite your musings in loftier terms. Let your thoughts flow in their own direction, capturing the emotion of the moment. Using a spiral notebook or legal pad allows you the freedom to scribble away.

For optimal results, practice these exercises for several weeks at least two or three minutes a day, every day. If you suffer from writer's block, don't sweat it. Tape-recording your thoughts can be very effective. The focal point of the exercise is the intent to "know thyself."

- Who am I? (Try reaching back as far as you can into childhood to remember the original dreams and desires of that child. We have quite often taken many steps away from our true self in the quest for approval and attention.)
- What do I want? What am I willing to do to get it?
- Whom do I need to forgive?
- What do I need to forgive myself for?
- What are my beliefs about being female/male?
- How do I allow guilt to control my life?

- What do I fear? How and to whom do I give my power away?
- What makes me angry? (Since anger is frequently linked to a time when we gave up our power, look for power leakages. Often we give up power out of fear or in exchange for approval.)
- What are my strengths?
- What are the attributes I like best about myself?
- How can I fully embrace who I am and appreciate my uniqueness?
- How can I walk my talk?
- What is my overriding passion?
- How can I be more fully alive?
- How can I create beauty with my life?
- What brings me joy?

Try also writing about these topics: money, failure, success, sex, men, women, relationships.

What you discover about your beliefs in this writing exercise can be used to reconstruct a new healthy belief in your body-mind link. Create a positive single statement for each subject to replace the old dysfunctional belief. You may want to share your writing with a sibling, friend, therapist, or personal group. The results can be amazing!

The Should/Could Exercise

This language exercise offers the opportunity for some amazing emancipation. The word *should* implies guilt, responsibility, inadequacy, and obligation. Still, we use this word constantly in our vocabulary without realizing its profound effect.

Make a list of all of your *shoulds.* Jot them down during the day when you catch yourself saying or thinking them. Here are some common ones: "I should work harder." "I should be a better person." "I should call Mom more often." "I should be more like my brother." Next, evaluate where these directives came from. Did they come from your aunt Alice, your mom or dad, your sixth-grade teacher, or are they your own? If you recognize that these *shoulds* are not your own, try this: Write them on individual pieces of paper, then rip them up or burn them and watch them go up in smoke. The point is they are not yours, so why tote them around?

Now, take the list of shoulds that still remain with you and rewrite them, beginning each sentence with "I could ..." The word *could* implies possibilities without the heavy feelings of guilt and duty. Allow the sense of obligation and responsibility to melt away and open your eyes to a whole new world of possibilities.

Child Collage

This exercise helps change the unhealthy messages that may have been planted long ago. Find a photo of yourself as a child at the age that needs the most attention. Get a large piece of poster board and place the photo in the center using adhesive or photograph corners to secure your photo. Then, for a couple of minutes each day, using pictures from magazines and newspapers and/or personal drawings, give that child everything he or she ever wanted. Remember, there is an aspect of every age in your adult being. Under certain conditions and stresses, you are likely to revert to that wounded age. With this exercise you can go back in time and give that child the gifts and symbols of love you did not get the first time around. It is never too late to reparent that child. Today is a great day to make the commitment to be a safe and loving parent to your child within.

Altar to Honor the Inner Child

Collect photos of yourself as a child at various ages and place them in a multiphoto frame or mount them on a poster board, being mindful of your precious photos. Be sure that the ages at which you felt most vulnerable or wounded are represented. Find a nightstand, table, or shelf to create a private altar. Make sure that this area won't be disturbed for several weeks. Cover the area with a pretty scarf or a beautiful piece of fabric. Place the photo collage on the altar. Gather and surround the photos with objects that speak of honoring (flowers, candles, incense, crystals, sacred art and objects, etc.) and comfort (favorite childhood toys, games, baseball cards, stuffed animals, your favorite blankie, etc.).

It's great if you can use actual objects from the past. After my mother passed away and her house was sold, I spent an afternoon cleaning out the attic before the new owners arrived. Behind an old dust-covered mattress, I found my love-worn collection of dolls and a dollhouse with furniture. I took them home with me and used them to build an altar that is both tactile and powerfully present. If you don't have any mementos of the past, don't sweat it. Gather things that represent your best-loved treasures. Take a few moments a day to visit this altar and look into your child's eyes and say I love you. The purpose of the exercise is to give a safe place where the child is loved, honored, listened to, and respected. Like the previous exercise, this is another opportunity to become a safe parent to the child within.

Family of the Heart

As children we are often limited to the family we were born to. As an adult we have more choices. We add spouses, children, and even friends to create a new extended family. Some Native Americans perform an adoption ritual when welcoming someone special into their family, waving a horsetail over the two people who are to be joined in a relationship. To this culture, horses symbolize freedom and are a reminder to stay free-flowing, never confining or limiting one another. If our family cannot accept us for who we are, or if we are living at a great geographical distance, joining with a family of the heart can provide a kinship that nurtures us.

Whether you are consciously choosing a healthier family or extending the family you already have, make a celebration out of it. Prepare a room with flowers and other decorations reflecting a joyful occasion. Share small but special gifts that symbolize what you like most about the new family member. If you are fresh out of horsetails, make something that represents the same idea. Smudging with the sacred smoke of sage and cedar can provide a symbol of unity. Whatever you choose, celebrate your newfound family of the heart with a ceremony of beauty.

Have You Had Your Hugs Today?

While children frequently find it easy to collect daily hugs from playmates, teachers, and parents, adults may find their hug quota seriously lacking. Still, the simple act of hugging has been confirmed as a miracle prescription for lowering blood pressure, raising hemoglobin, boosting the immune system, and generally reducing stress. At the renowned Menninger Foundation, hugging has effectively been used to treat patients who suffer from depression. It is widely believed to prolong life and increase energy.

In the home, a couple of hugs a day can improve family dynamics and keep divorce court at bay. If you live alone, a hug from friends can fill your touch quota nicely. Don't be shy. Reach out and hug someone. The huggee will benefit from it as much as you do. A pet can step in when a friend is not available. We respond to the affectionate nuzzling of a pet just as a pet responds to our gentle touch.

The variety of hug you choose is purely personal. Here's a list of silly ways to snuggle up. There is the *getting acquainted hug,* whereby you gently grasp the huggee's shoulders with heads touching briefly. There is absolutely no body contact below the shoulders. This one is great for your mother-in-law, blind dates, and Aunt Josie. Take a chance with the *heartfelt granny hug.* Start with arms fully wrapped around the huggee's shoulders and move in to a full cheek contact, swaying gently back and forth for a good minute. For your more intimate acquaintances, go for the *full-body contact hug.* Begin with direct eye contact. Then move in confidently for the full-frontal meld. The truly daring may fancy the style of their French cousins. Embrace at the elbow and kiss each other's cheeks continuously until you are exhausted. Men may prefer the *sports hug,* which includes three quick pats on the shoulder and an occasional "I love you, man." Whatever your style, hugging brightens everyone's day. So reach out and hug someone!

Reflect on your radiant face in the mirror. Gather your *shoulds* and throw them to the wind. Build a beautiful altar for re-creating a beautiful you. Journal your beliefs. Bring a funny story to your next staff meeting and inflate the room with laughter. Fill your hug quota and brighten up your day. Make a commitment to change the outmoded patterns of your subconscious mind and truly become the author of your life.

Chapter 7

Meditation

Don't Just Sit There ... Meditate!

THE SUN RISES out of the ocean. A soft yellow light embraces me as it reaches across the surface of the steel-blue water. Waves lap gently at my feet. A light breeze carries the musical sound of birds singing a salute to the sun, and white sand molds softly beneath me. I breathe deeply, inhaling as the waves advance and exhaling as the waves gently roll back to the sea. I am one with the universe. My cassette recording of ocean sounds clicks off, letting me know my time is up. I open my eyes. The sun has risen and is shining through the icy mosaic of my living room window. The noise of my children arguing surfaces, drowning out the annoying repetitious background hum of the dishwasher. It's all music to my ears. I stand and stretch, renewed, refreshed, confident that I am ready for whatever the day may bring. For deep inside me, I hold the image of my quiet place, my daily meditation, that will carry me peacefully throughout the day.

The Mind Has the Power to Heal

If you think meditation means a dark room filled with long-haired gurus sporting love beads, surrounded by swirling incense, think again. The concept of meditation has come a long way since its cultural introduction in the 1970s.

In fact, meditation has hit the mainstream. Although traditionally a spiritual practice, meditation is now being recognized as a powerful tool for gaining and maintaining health. Legions of physicians are prescribing meditation along with medication for patients suffering from autoimmune diseases such as cancer. Psychotherapists are using meditation to assist patients in healing old traumas and achieving a sense of self-awareness and self-control. Sports trainers are including meditation in their programs to fine-tune an athlete's concentration and increase reaction time. Even corporate America is offering meditation instructions to their executives to maintain employee health, hone alertness and creativity, and increase productivity.

Meditation has hit the streets. Everybody's doing it. Here's why.

Waking the Physician Within

As far back as 1968, when physicians at Harvard Medical School found that a practice of meditation resulted in significant physiological benefits, physicians and scientists alike have been investigating the power of meditation. Clinical studies have shown meditation can decrease both respiration and heart rates, lower blood pressure, balance the endocrine system, improve arterial health, and strengthen the nervous system. With meditation, positive changes occur in the brain. Meditation can lessen the amount of cortisol in the bloodstream, a major stress hormone that can damage the memory center of the brain, while increasing alpha waves, the brain waves associated with relaxation. By improving neurotransmitter function and cerebral blood flow, meditation can induce mental clarity and improve areas of mental function, including memory and IQ.

Meditation has been found to significantly decrease chronic pain especially in patients with stress-related disorders. At the Stress Reduction Clinic at the University of Massachusetts along with hundreds of other clinics across the nation, instructions on meditation are offered to help patients let go of their tension and runaway thoughts of pain and instead become an objective observer of them. The results are fewer doctor visits and less medication.

At the renowned Menninger Foundation, meditation techniques are used to enhance immune systems in patients suffering from autoimmune diseases, AIDS, and cancer, as well as people with drug and alcohol addictions. One clinical study found that cancer survivors lived five times longer than expected when involved with group support, meditation therapy, and other spiritual practices.

Meditation can aid in a patient's recovery process. Often, the emotions associated with illness or injury, such as fear, worry, and depression, can impede the healing process, actually causing further damage to muscles and tissue and suppressing the immune system. Meditation can break this emotional pattern, allowing the patient to relax and calm the nervous system, assisting the body's own healing powers.

Practitioners are utilizing the benefits of meditation when treating PMS, hot flashes, even infertility. Studies discovered that after practicing a form of relaxation therapy or meditation, 60 percent of women experienced reduced PMS symptoms. By reducing stress that can disrupt women's ovulation cycles and that can reduce the sperm count in men, clinics are successfully using relaxation programs to help couples conceive.

Psychotherapy and meditation are combining forces to help patients recover from debilitating fear, depression, anxiety, phobias, obsessive-compulsive disorders, panic attacks, and insomnia. A Harvard psychologist discovered that relaxation therapy helped 75 percent of his long-term insomniac patients fall asleep within twenty minutes. Many people turn to psychotherapy when they feel emotionally and creatively blocked or are overwhelmed with feelings of isolation and fear. Combining a meditative approach with traditional psychotherapy can help patients learn to let go of their thought processes, reduce stress, and balance their highs and lows. By practicing present-time awareness, they can lessen worry and fear about the past or future.

Meditation aids people suffering from depression by guiding them to become aware of their negative thought patterns and let go of them, while focusing on positive, peaceful images or mantras. Meditation is also used to assist patients in healing old traumas by teaching them to detach from old memories. Patients learn that although their lives may remain the same, their attitudes toward how they interpret their lives have changed.

Meditation may even help you live longer. People who practice meditation over an extended period of time not only experience improved health but have actually shown increased levels of DHEA, a hormone associated with youth and immune function, which reduces the body's core temperature, increases memory, and preserves sexual function. Depleted levels of DHEA have been strongly linked to Alzheimer's disease. In addition, meditation can have a notable effect on the three primary indicators of aging: vision and hearing loss, and elevated blood pressure.

In all cases, meditation has been recognized as a profound technique to help the body's inner intelligence to restore homeostasis and to assist in self-healing.

Happiness Is an Inside Job

Living life at today's harried pace is taking its toll. Most of us spend our time on automatic pilot, exhausted, creatively spent, focusing on the future or dwelling on the past. Our minds are overrun with an army of thoughts that float through our consciousness every minute, filling our brain with clutter, pulling us in a hundred directions at once.

To keep up with life in the fast lane, we have learned to rely heavily on our beta consciousness, or our linear, analytical mind. Beta functions include writing, reading, math, our relationship to time, and cause-and-effect thinking. They allow us to dissect elements of the whole and organize them in a linear manner, making it easier to compute different data at the same time. Beta consciousness is often a necessary device to cope in today's world, where multitasking has become a survival tool in the workplace and at home.

With our concentration on beta thinking, we have sorely neglected our inner consciousness, which is filled with non-linear alpha, theta, and delta brain waves. It is this consciousness that allows us to deeply relax; center our awareness; get in touch with our creativity and spontaneity; make broad, sweeping connections instead of categorizing information; and see life as a whole. Children live primarily at the alpha level.

Also, as we learned in Chapter 6, our thought processes are often controlled by our subconscious mind, which has been patterned early on in our lives by society, family, and peers. When left unattended, the mind can often be a harsh taskmaster, making judgments about every action, criticizing, and creating an oppressive cloud of contradicting thoughts.

Frequently, what happens in the world outside ourselves has little to do with our reaction to it. The colors, sounds, people, and events of the outside world exist only when they are registered internally, passing through the filters of our sensory system, identified and understood by our mind. We get so accustomed to this process of identifying and interpreting that we forget it is constantly taking place. It is our *inner* mind that judges the events of our lives, having control over how we feel about them. In other words, happiness is an inside job.

Meditation allows us to leap into this inner world, tapping primarily into an alpha state, the threshold between the inner and outer consciousness. By learning to look at our repeated thoughts and patterns objectively, noting them, counting and labeling them, we become the observer of how our inner mind works without delving into the contents of each thought that passes through.

Physical Responses to Stress

To add to the chaos, our biological makeup frequently works against us. The instinctual brain, a carryover from our reptilian and tree-dwelling ancestors, still primarily controls our reaction to stress. Often our body, muscles, and hormones react with a fight-or-flight response to any stressful situation without us even thinking about it. In the days of the cave dwellers, it was key to our survival.

In our modern world, however, situations of stress are generally less life threatening. Yet our instinctual brain continues to react to life's constant challenges, such as financial worries, family problems, scheduling conflicts, or simply being late for an appointment, as if our life depended on it. Because stress is cumulative, a seemingly small event can trigger a huge response. Unlike our ancestors, we regularly lack the physical response, such as fighting or running away, needed to burn up this energy, allowing the hormones to subside. Instead, our bodies remain awash with adrenaline and the stress hormone cortisol, a combination that interferes with the function of the key t4 cells of the immune system, lowering our resistance to many diseases, from viruses to cancer.

What can we do to bring our mind and therefore our lives under control? The answer is simple. *Meditate.*

Using this self-directed practice of quieting the mind and relaxing the body, we can counteract the fight-or-flight response by activating the parasympathetic nervous system. No one can control the events that happen in the world. What we can change is our mental and therefore our physical reaction to these events.

What Is Meditation, Anyway?

It may surprise you to know that we meditate throughout the day without recognizing it. Meditation requires focusing our awareness on one thing. Whenever we focus our mind on a project, situation, or thought so that no other thoughts can intervene, we enter an alpha state of mind. In other words, we meditate. Swinging golf clubs can be a meditation, playing the guitar, practicing yoga, even baking a pie.

Meditation is simply the art of mental self-control. Focusing on our breath, a vision, an object, or a mantra allows us to still the chatter of our mind. By learning to ignore the hundreds of thoughts that float through our consciousness every minute, we can bring the mind into present-moment awareness, leaving the stressful memories of the past or plans for the future behind. With the practice of meditation, we can become better equipped to handle the stress of our everyday lives, sitting next to the frenzied external world without losing our center.

The study of meditation does not have to be painful or tedious. Meditation is not difficult to learn. In fact, it's quite simple. With the exercises provided later in this chapter, you can enjoy this practice anywhere: in the doctor's office, at your desk, or in the sanctuary of your home.

Types of Meditation

There are many types of meditation. In this chapter, we will explore a variety of techniques that are great for beginners or those in need of a refresher. You may want to seek out a teacher or group as your practice advances. Included are exercises using concentrative meditation—techniques that focus the mind on breath, imagery, or sound (mantra) meditations as well as the mindfulness approach. We will also delve into the movement meditations, including the walking meditation of the Zen Buddhists. Finally, since meditation is found in all major religions, we will examine a technique for devotional meditation.

Whether you are addressing a health problem or want to increase your powers of concentration, improve self-acceptance, deepen your connection to your creativity, or just relax, try meditation. It can take you there, simply.

Meditation Exercises

Preparation

- Set aside five to twenty minutes per day. Even a few minutes a day is helpful. Most of the techniques described here are designed to take five minutes to complete.
- Turn off the phone, lock the door, put the cat out—whatever assures you a few glorious quiet moments. This is your time. Take it.
- Try meditating on an empty stomach. Meditating after a big lunch may find you napping at your desk just when your boss passes by. Meditating first thing in the morning is best since the stress hormone cortisol is often at elevated levels. First wash your hands and face to ward off sleepiness.
- Meditation is like a physical workout and it helps to have a physical place set aside to do it. Whether in a room or corner of your house, set an atmosphere. You may want to light a candle, diffuse some aromatherapy oils, or put

on some soft music. Add some sacred artwork or pictures of beings who inspire you.

- Wear comfortable clothing. Sit on the floor cross-legged or in a chair with both feet on the floor, back straight but not rigid. There is no need to force your body into a lotus position, mirroring Indian *yogis*. That's just the way Indians sit. Instead choose a comfortable position that's right for you, being mindful that a straight spine keeps you alert and helps conduct the energy of your breath during the meditation period.

- Hand placements, or *mudras*, embody different energies. Try palms down on your knees when you are feeling self-contained. Palms up on your knees stimulates receptivity. Hands clasped together generates revolving and contained energy. Choose a hand placement according to how you feel.

- Take a few deep breaths before you begin and continue them throughout the meditation. Relax your body, releasing tension held in your muscles with each exhalation. As in yoga, deep breathing is a fundamental component of meditation.

- Practice with regularity. A five- to twenty-minute daily practice at the same time each day is best for beginners. Try twice a day when you are more comfortable with the methods.

Counting Breath Meditation

The counting breath meditation is a great way to begin a practice. With this simple concentration technique, observing the inhalations and exhalations of your breath, you can learn to focus the mind and achieve onepointedness.

Close your eyes and breathe deeply. You may want to use the *pranayama* breath explored in Chapters 4 and 5. Feel the sensation of your breath filling your body with life-giving energy, then exhale fully. Now, mentally count your breaths: inhale ... after exhaling, count *one*, inhale ... exhale, *two*, concentrating only on the sensation of your breath and the counting. When you reach the count of five, go back and begin the cycle again. When outside thoughts come in (and they will) refocus on the sensation of your breath and your counting. If you lose count, just start again. As you become more familiar with this method, try counting to ten and then twenty without being interrupted by busy thoughts.

Simple Chore Breath Counting Meditation

Now that you are familiar with the breath counting meditation, try this. The simple chore breath allows you to meditate while performing an action. This practice is a favorite among Zen Buddhists, who believe that concentration on the ordinary in daily life adds to it the *extraordinary*. By paying attention to daily chores such as eating, sleeping, cooking, working, and walking, Zen Buddhists offer these actions as prayers, thus rendering sacred the ordinary parts of life.

The next time you are doing a mindless task or function that you do on a regular basis, count the breaths it takes you to complete the task. When you make a run to the copy machine or to the bus stop to pick up your kids, when you are making a cup of tea or pot of soup, remain focused on counting your breath until you complete your task. When thoughts invade, turn your attention back to the job of accurately counting your breaths. Start out with short, easy tasks. Later you may want to try counting while performing more complicated tasks.

The Heartbeat Meditation

Here is another exercise that helps you learn to focus your mind. Sit comfortably cross-legged or in a chair. Take several deep, cleansing breaths. When you are ready, place your hand over your heart or on the pulse point of your wrist. Now, count the beat of your heart to the count of five, ten, or twenty, without being distracted, as you learned in the counting breath exercise. Try to concentrate on only the beating of your heart. If thoughts come in and interrupt you, begin again. Try this for five minutes or so a day. It is a great way to reconnect with yourself and know that you are truly alive.

Outside/Inside Meditation

During the winter months or year-round in our offices, we are often trapped inside, losing our vital connection with nature. Here's a meditation that lets you bring the outside in.

Sit near a window or in front of a picture that represents a beautiful nature scene: the endless ocean, a colorful sunset, a tranquil lake, or majestic mountains. Look at this scene for a few minutes. Now, close your eyes and picture it mentally. Drawing the image into your mind's eye, see it in great detail. Explore the scene thoroughly, hear the sounds, breathe in the aromas, feel the sun or wind on your face. Continue your breath while you observe the natural beauty around you. After a few minutes, open your eyes and enjoy the renewing force of the nature within.

The Flame Meditation

This simple exercise can help you learn to focus your mind by honing your awareness of a single object. Sit cross-legged on your cushion or in a chair with a lit candle on a table about a foot in front of you at eye level. Take several deep cleansing breaths and release the tension in your shoulders, neck, and wherever else you are holding it. Now, concentrate on the center, or heart, of the flame. Thoughts will begin to float up in you about the day, the room you're in, the sounds that surround you. Each time your mind wanders, refocus your awareness on the flame. After a minute or two, blow out the flame and close your eyes. You'll see the image of the flame dance behind your eyelids. Concentrate on it. Watch how it moves, changes color, burns with a cool warmth.

The flame meditation is good training for the mindfulness meditation that follows. By learning to focus, you also learn to let go of your thought processes.

Mindfulness Meditation

Mindfulness is the act of being fully aware of what happens in each moment. In this meditation, you remain alert, allowing thoughts to rise to the surface, being aware of them without judging them or interpreting their contents.

Sit comfortably on a cushion or in a chair. Close your eyes. Take several cleansing breaths. When thoughts arise, let them, without delving into their meaning. Simply say the word "thinking" whenever thoughts appear. You'll find that without your attachment to these thoughts, they won't stick around long. To sharpen the focus of your meditation, you can label your thoughts *past, future, planning, fantasy, worrying,* and so on, as they pass through. Then simply release them and watch them fade away.

Walking Meditation

Walking meditation is an exercise in mindfulness. By adding movement to meditation, you can expand your practice to include it wherever you go. The way you stand, the way you walk, the way you eat or even work out can all be forms of meditation that bring awareness into your life.

First, choose an area where you can walk at least ten feet in one direction. Then begin walking slowly, hands stationary at your sides, eyes straight ahead, focusing your attention on each position of the foot as you walk: lifting, forward motion as it moves through the air, and placement of the foot on the ground. Complete one footstep before lifting the other foot. Say the words "lifting, moving, planting" repeatedly to keep your mind focused on the action. When you first attempt this meditation, take at least eight to ten seconds to complete each step. With this meditation you can quiet your mind while bringing your full attention to the experience of walking.

Simple Chanting (Mantra) Meditation

The practice of repeating a mantra, a word or spiritual saying, over and over offers a powerful healing tool due to the vibratory effect of sound. (See Chapter 1.) Vibrations from mantras can stimulate the part of the endocrine system located in the head and neck, including the master glands of the pituitary and hypothalamus. In addition, repetition of a sound or word allows the mind to concentrate on one thought, one pulse of energy, disconnecting it from conscious thought. You can practice this method for a few minutes as part of your daily healing ritual or while doing something as mundane as standing in the checkout line. There are many mantras to choose from. Here are some examples and what they invoke:

- OM—forces of creation
- Ong—creator
- The Lord Is My Shepherd—protective powers of God
- Shalom—peace
- Sat Nam—the truth is my identity
- Namaste—I salute the divinity within
- Sa Ta Na Ma—birth, life, death, rebirth
- Hail Mary Full of Grace—prayer to the blessed Virgin Mary
- Amen—unity
- Aum—oneness

You can choose one of these mantras or any other that you feel connected with. Using beads or rosaries to keep track of your mantras can help. The tactileness of the beads and the moving of the hands give the mind an additional focal point.

Devotional Chanting

Chanting mantras, praying, and singing to the beloved are all forms of devotional meditation, which is a practice found in all major religions. Sacred chants have been found in the oral traditions of indigenous tribes dating back to their beginnings. The benefits derived from devotional chanting are numerous. Repeating the name of the divine helps slow respiration, retune the body with extended vowel sounds (typically found in devotional chants), and fulfill our desire to merge with the divine.

Begin by sitting with a picture, statue, or icon of a divine being, whether it is Jesus, Buddha, Isis, Quan Yin, Krishna, or another deity of your choice. Now, after a few moments of gazing at your beloved, visualize this being as moving into your body and sitting in your heart or heart chakra. Know that this being loves you unconditionally, despite your faults and weaknesses. See yourself reflected in the unwavering compassion of this being, bathed in tranquillity and unconditional love. You may use a mantra, specific sound, short prayer, or devotional name to stay focused. Since this is a devotional meditation it's important that you choose a prayer or mantra that is right for you. At the end of the meditation, allow the unconditional love that resides in your heart to flow outward.

By holding these beings in your heart, you are filled with their loving qualities. After doing this meditation, you may find that these qualities become your own, sparking the divinity within.

❖ ❖ ❖

Meditation is a search for enlightenment, an enlightenment that lies in the journey of everyday life. It's in the journey toward enlightenment that we experience life at its fullest. It's in the journey that we have all the fun. So the next time you're stuck in traffic, in the waiting room of the dentist's office, or waking up to a new day, don't just sit there ... meditate.

Chapter 8

Chakras

A Layperson's Guide

AS SO FREQUENTLY HAPPENS in my life, I was introduced to the world of chakras in a whirlwind fashion. After attending a workshop given by a well-known healer, to my surprise I was picked out of the crowd and asked to become her assistant during her road tour. Within a weekend's time, I was taken from A to Z in the master's course in chakras, never to return to ordinary reality again. This began a three-year chapter in my life during which I witnessed remarkable transformations of body, mind, and soul, fueling my desire to understand this mysterious system. I have spent the last twenty years exploring and incorporating this knowledge of the chakras and realized that, like our bodies, *The 5-Minute Healer* would not be complete without them.

History and Mythology of the Chakras

Evidence of the chakra system dates back to Sanskrit tablets from 6000 B.C. Knowledge of this system has been found in many traditions such as Chinese Taoism, Tibetan Buddhism, African Bushmen, and some Native American cultures. Chakras were most fully explored by the Hindus of India some four thousand years ago through art, symbols, and allegorical myths. In Hindu mythology, the chakra system is represented by Shakti, the goddess of the material universe, and Shiva, the god of the unmanifest universe. Shakti ascends from the earth and Shiva descends from the heavens as they reach out to embrace each other. The myth proclaims that through their embrace Shiva impregnates Shakti, bringing life force and consciousness together. In another Hindu myth, the latent power of the chakra system is represented by the goddess Kundalini, who coils at the base of the spine three and one-half times. When awakened, this serpent goddess surges upward through the chakras, releasing blockages and opening awareness.

Research

Until recently, Western society has lacked physical evidence of the spiritual energy of the body, the energy found in the aura, chakras, and subtle body. Over the past several decades, however, researchers have identified and proven that the energy field produced by the body and the chakra system is both real and measurable.

Through the discoveries of quantum physics, we have come to understand that everything alive is made up of energy and information. The human body and its physiological processes produce electromagnetic fields. We are surrounded by this energy field, often referred to as the *aura,* from head to toe, extending several feet from our bodies. This energy field remains in constant exchange with the outside world.

An extensive research project conducted at UCLA offered quantitative proof that the aura and chakras did indeed exist. During this experiment, electrodes connected to an oscilloscope were attached to the chakras and acupuncture points of the patients. Measurements of energies moving through the body, as well as frequencies equating to particular colors, were recorded. One of the amazing conclusions of this research is that chakras are real and quantitative, radiate a color, and transmit measurable frequencies in the body.

Russian scientists have been experimenting with the relationship between the chakras and our emotions for decades. Through the use of Kirlian photography, a proven photographic technique allowing us to view light emanations from plants, animals, and humans, Russian experiments recorded energy leakages emanating from the different areas of the body associated with chakras. Photographs of a subject who is calm and even-tempered showed minimal flares of light radiating from the subject's body. Recording an emotionally tense person revealed bright flares emanating from the subject's body, offering visual proof that chakras respond by altering their size and shape to various emotional and physical situations.

Chakras: What Are They, Anyway?

Chakra is a Sanskrit word meaning "rotating or spinning wheel." These spinning wheels of energy are located in the *subtle body*, an energy field that surrounds us and is superimposed on the physical body. Chakras reside at the core of the subtle body, radiating out from the center of the spinal cord and appearing as spinning disks of light, each emitting a specific color. There are seven major chakras, which follow the front of the spinal column and connect with the endocrine glands and nerve ganglia. Additional powerful chakras are located in the hands and feet. There are also many minor chakras located at the joints of the body, such as shoulders, knees, hips, ankles, wrists, and elbows.

The energy of the chakras moves constantly, traveling a bidirectional path between our inner selves and the outer world, feeding us information and energy. In addition, through the breath, kundalini energy travels two currents, *ida* and *pingala,* feeding the chakras' vital life force. Both the *ida* and the *pingala* move from the base of the spine upward, the *pingala* traveling on the right and *ida* on the left. Some studies show that these channels are connected with the sympathetic and parasympathetic nervous systems.

Experiencing Chakras

We experience our chakra system every day whether or not we are aware of it. When we are in a heightened emotional state or are experiencing a noticeable physical response, the chakra system becomes almost discernible. These simple examples can better illustrate our connection with this invisible system.

Imagine this: You are standing in front of your company's CEOs at a year-end meeting, about to give a project report about a new program you have spearheaded. You step to the podium, your hands clammy, your knees weak, and suddenly you feel your throat close as you attempt to speak. *You are experiencing your throat chakra constricting.*

When confronted with an unexpected verbal assault, have you ever felt as if you had been kicked in the stomach? *This is the result of shock registering in the solar plexus.*

Who hasn't experienced the feeling of a "broken heart," an actual pain in the chest from the loss of a loved one? *This is the heart chakra closing because of emotional pain from grief and loss.*

You can conduct your own experiment to experience the tangibility of these energy centers. With arms shoulder distance apart and elbows bent, begin compressing the energy that flows from the palm chakras, gently patting the air in all directions with palms facing each other, as if you were patting an invisible basketball. Continue, slowly moving your palms closer together, feeling the energy build up until you sense a pulsating energy ball, a magnetic field, the size of a baseball, between your palms. This demonstrates the invisible energies that surround our body and radiate from the hand chakras. Although we cannot see this energy, it is nonetheless a vital part of us.

How Do Chakras Affect Us?

Consider the relationship of the chakras and the physical body as an integral network, a complex telecommunication system that constantly shares information and energy. As we stated before, we experience a two-way informational exchange between our inner self and the outer world. Each chakra connects with a specific nerve ganglia and area of the endocrine system in the body that affects both physical and emotional processes. The chakra system is both physical and nonphysical, material and nonmaterial, connecting the body and spirit together, creating what we call the body-mind link.

A three-way interrelationship exists between our physiology, our emotions, and the seven major chakras. This interrelationship is not a new idea. As we have learned in previous chapters, our thoughts and emotions have a profound effect on our body's immune, central nervous, and endocrine systems. We also know that a repeated illness can influence our thoughts, making us depressed, anxiety-ridden, feeling hopeless. Now overlay the chakras. The health of the seven major chakras influences who we are and what we think and feel. In good health, our chakras are open, radiate pure color, enliven health, and lend a clearer perspective on our relationship with the world and ourselves. In turn, an unhealthy chakra system will adversely affect the way we interpret information from our environment and can cause disharmony in the body at a cellular level. It is the barometer by which we measure our relationship with self and the world.

Each chakra governs a specific area of the body connected with particular endocrine glands and nerve plexuses in that area. A physical condition such as arthritis may result in a disfigured root or first chakra. A heart or fourth chakra blockage may suggest heart or lung congestion. A stomach ulcer will certainly result in a dense solar plexus or third chakra.

Because the chakras are not only physical but also metaphysical, there are specific psychological and spiritual processes associated with each. An emotional condition such as a feeling of inferiority will register in the third chakra. An inability to let go of the past or an abundance of negative thinking could result in congestion in the root chakra. Shyness or a fear of public speaking might manifest in an undeveloped throat chakra.

Which came first, the emotion, the physical condition, or the chakra disorder? Who knows? When illness or imbalance does occur, it's crucial not to judge yourself or your body unfairly. Illness is merely an indicator, a teacher, allowing us to listen to the innate intelligence of the body. Often, it is our limiting belief patterns, frequently given to us by our culture, that create the imbalance initially. As we develop and grow from childhood, so do our chakras. Much of the input from our original households impacts not only our emotional state but the chakra system itself. For example, if we are raised with the belief that children should be seen but not heard, our ability to use our throat chakra will be affected, limiting our ability to speak our truth. If we are exposed to physical abuse, it will influence our first chakra, disturbing our feeling of safety in the world and the ability to be fully grounded and alive. Other components, such as an unhealthy diet, lack of exercise, pollution, physical injury, and emotional trauma, can also profoundly influence a healthy system. Maintaining a healthy chakra system is fundamentally important in the maintenance of our relationship to ourselves and the world around us.

This figure offers a visual description of each area in which the chakras reside and the functions that are most often accredited to them.

The chakras and their function

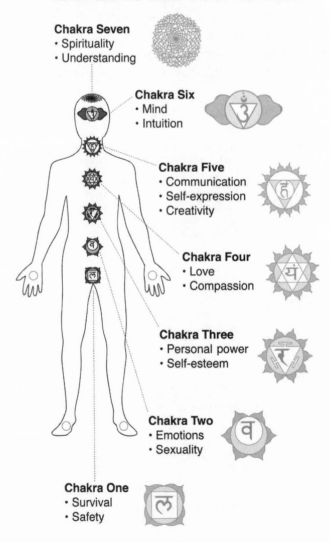

Chakra Seven
- Spirituality
- Understanding

Chakra Six
- Mind
- Intuition

Chakra Five
- Communication
- Self-expression
- Creativity

Chakra Four
- Love
- Compassion

Chakra Three
- Personal power
- Self-esteem

Chakra Two
- Emotions
- Sexuality

Chakra One
- Survival
- Safety

Exercises for Balancing the Chakras

Tuning Up

Instead of studying Sanskrit tablets dating back to 6000 B.C., this chapter provides the layperson's guide to the chakras. Throughout this book, I have included exercises that directly affect and help balance the chakra system found in the yoga, sound, color, aromatherapy, meditation, and breathing chapters. The exercises in this chapter complete your owner's manual

Chakra (Sanskrit) Element	Physical Location	Functions Governed
Root/1st (Muladhara) Earth	Perineum, sciatic nerve, coccygeal plexus, testicles	Survival, grounding, security, life force, rootedness
Sacral/2nd (Svadhisthana) Water	Ovaries, uterus, sacral plexus, intestines, small of back, Peyer's patches*	Emotions, desires, relationships, creativity
Solar plexus/3rd (Manipura) Fire	Solar plexus, pancreas, adrenals, stomach, liver	Power, will, self-confidence
Heart/4th (Anahata) Air	Heart, lungs, cardiac and pulmonary plexuses, thymus	Love, compassion, forgiveness
Throat/5th (Visshudha) Ether/sound	Throat, ears, parathyroid, thyroid, pharyngeal plexus, shoulders, mouth	Communication, expression, creativity
Third Eye/6th (Ajna) Mind/Light	Pituitary, eyes, lower brain, carotid plexus	Inspiration, intuition, wisdom, inner vision
Crown/7th (Sahasrara) Cosmos/spirit	Pineal, upper brain, cerebral cortex	Spirituality, sense of purpose, bliss

*Peyer's patches, found in the interstitial cells of the intestinal wall and appendix, are connected with the body's immune system.

of chakra repair. Use the table and techniques to help balance the chakras and give yourself a tune-up that will carry you harmoniously through the day.

Gem Therapy

You can use the chart to better understand the location of the chakras and the concepts and emotions they govern. Then try experimenting with gem therapy. Our bodies are made up of carbon and metallic components that are also present in various

Gemstone	Color	Musical Note and Mantra
Red garnet, ruby, carnelian, hematite, tiger's eye, obsidian	Red	C LAM
Citrine, aquamarine, bloodstone, red jasper	Orange	D VAM
Topaz, amber, aragonite	Yellow	E RAM
Emerald, green tourmaline, rose quartz	Green	F YAM
Sapphire, turquoise, blue lace agate	Blue	G HAM
Lapis, azurite, sugilite, labradorite	Indigo	A AUM or OM
Diamond, amethyst, clear quartz, herkimer	Violet**	B SILENCE

**White light, the merging of all colors, appears above the crown chakra.

gems, metals, and plants. When placed directly on the skin, these gemstones and metals exert an electromagnetic influence on the energy centers (chakras) and the physical cells of the body, helping to bring them into balance.

Let the Music Play

Punch a note out on your piano, electronic keyboard, pitch pipe, guitar, or harmonica. Begin with the root chakra note, middle C. Add your voice, holding the note until you feel it vibrate in that chakra location. Let that note wash over your body. After a minute or two, continue up the scale until you have reached B, the note of the seventh chakra. Now you are vibrating in harmony.

Grounding Exercise

This exercise helps to reconnect the root chakra and chakras in the feet (extensions of the root chakra) to the energy of the earth while rebalancing the entire chakra system. During a hectic day, we tend to build up tensions and an excess of mental activity, becoming scattered and disconnected. Reconnecting to the earth allows us to discharge this excess energy into the ground, restoring balance and clarity.

Begin by sitting on a chair or stool with your bare feet resting on the floor. If weather allows, go outside and sit on a bench, rock, or the ground, resting your back against a tree. Your feet need to be flat on the ground, connected to the earth. Slowly feel your body settle into this space, feeling the gentle force of gravity reconnecting you to the earth. Take several deep breaths, relaxing into this earth connection. Release all tension from your body. Noticing your feet, lightly press your heels into the ground or floor. Feel the energy flow from your tailbone down to your feet and into the earth, much as a tree extends its roots deeply into the soil.

Relaxing into this comfortable heaviness, visualize your tail-bone or base of the spine as your taproot connecting deeply with the earth. This taproot is your root chakra. Now align the top of your head, your throat, and the trunk of your body over the root chakra. Imagine a brilliant red light moving up from the ground through the central core of your root chakra and back down through the earth. Feel the tension leave your body and discharge harmlessly into the ground. Take several minutes to enjoy this reunion with the life-sustaining energies of the earth. When you feel complete, begin coming back to your surroundings. Wiggle your fingers and toes and when you are ready open your eyes. Now, feeling grounded and renewed, take this energy with you into your day.

Hands-On Technique

We often forget the healing power we have in our own bodies. With this technique, we will be using our own hands to balance our chakras.

Find a comfortable place on the floor, bed, or in a chair. Close your eyes and take several deep and relaxing breaths, loosening your neck, shoulders, chest, abdomen, and lower torso, all the way to your toes. Now, visualize a light coming from above your crown chakra, entering the top of your head and expanding to your chest, arms, hands, down through your lower body, and out your feet. Feeling the wonderful healing light tingle in your body, bring your attention to your hands, illuminating them with this healing light. Now, without opening your eyes, clasp your hands together over the root chakra or pubic bone, seeing the healing energies of the earth and natural world concentrated there. Leave your hands over the root chakra until you feel a current of energy running between your hands and the root chakra area. Continue moving your hands up the chakras until you feel each one balance and cleanse. Affirm in your mind that you are cleansing your body, mind, and soul.

When you are finished, imagine that your entire body is sealed in an ovoid of healing and protective golden light. Slowly, come back to the room by wiggling your toes and fingers, and when you are ready, open your eyes.

Mantras for What Ails You

Adding a mantra to your daily routine can help balance the energy of the chakras while stimulating the endocrine system with the vibrations of sound. Sit for five minutes, close your eyes, and repeat each mantra for a short time. Visualizing the correlating chakra, send the energy there. Or choose one chakra that you think needs attention and take a moment to recite a mantra for what ails you.

- Chakra 1   LAM (Oneness)
- Chakra 2   VAM (Love one another)
- Chakra 3   RAM (I honor myself)
- Chakra 4   YAM (Love is all)
- Chakra 5   HAM (I communicate truth)
- Chakra 6   OM (I perceive truth)
- Chakra 7   Silence (I am one with God)

Color Breathing

Color breathing is another exercise I use to realign myself with the world around me. To fully understand the power of color, refer to Chapter 2 on color therapy. Have someone read aloud the following exercise or record it so you can fully relax in the visualization. Begin by sitting in a comfortable chair or lying down on a carpeted floor or blanket. Take a deep breath through your nose, exhaling fully. Continue breathing deeply while you relax your shoulders and neck, then your arms, chest, pelvis, legs, and feet. Continue until you are fully relaxed.

With your next breath, imagine that the air you are breathing is a pure ruby or cherry red. With your eyes closed, see a fresh bowl of ripe, sour cherries before you. Visualizing red can be used as a grounding device connecting you with the earth. It helps with assertiveness, positivity, and motivation. Breathe the color red fully several times until you are ready to move on.

Next, imagine that the air you breathe is the pure color orange, seeing yourself picking a ripe, succulent orange from a tree full of the rich smell of orange blossoms. Take a deep breath and release. Breathing in orange stimulates the emotions and creates a feeling of well-being. It can also revitalize a tired body or combat muscle spasms or cramps. When you are feeling emotionally stuck, or unable to speak your "peace," direct the color orange to your throat. It can help dissolve the block. Breathe in orange until you are ready to continue.

Now imagine that the air you breathe is yellow. See yourself tasting the delicious juice of a fresh-cut lemon. Breathe in the color yellow and release, repeating several times. Yellow activates the motor nerves, stimulates energy in the muscles, and is beneficial to the skin. In some psychology circles, it has even been known to help alleviate depression. Breathing in yellow is a great pick-me-up.

Next, breathe in the color of emerald green. Imagine yourself entering a multifaceted emerald sparkling in the sunlight. Breathing green can restore harmony and balance in your life. It is nature's own tonic and exercises a strong and positive influence on the heart and blood supply. Green is the ultimate color of renewal. Breathe in green several times before moving on.

Now, imagine that the air that you breathe is sky-blue. See yourself lying on your back looking up at a crystal-clear sky.

Breathe in the color blue deeply, several times. Blue is the color of the throat chakra and can counter feverish or inflamed conditions. It has an antiseptic quality and produces a calm and restful effect. Breathe the color blue until you are ready to go on.

Next, breathe in the color indigo, a luxurious deep violet-blue. Imagine light is pouring through a handblown Venetian glass vase as you stand in front of it, absorbing the radiant indigo color. Breathing in indigo has a cooling effect. It can reduce bleeding and has even been known to help rid one of obsessions. Take several deep breaths of indigo before advancing to the next color.

Now, see yourself immersed in a field of violet-colored irises, drinking deeply of their color. Violet depresses the motor nerves and the lymphatic and cardiac systems. Breathe in the rich and airy color of violet several times and release. It is a color that should not be used when you are under emotional stress for it is very ungrounding. Using this color will send you further out of your body.

Finish by breathing in the color white, which allows you to merge all the colors together. Imagine you are watching a shimmering white dove soar above you. Breathe in that shimmering white color several times. Breathing in white quiets the chattering mind and can calm you before meditation or sleep. White, however, tends to take you out of your body and is not a good choice when you need to concentrate. Breathe in white several times before concluding.

If you don't have time to visualize all of these colors one at a time in the order presented, starting with red and ending with white, try breathing in the color you think you need most. When in doubt, use green for balance and harmony, orange to calm emotions, yellow for a mental pickup, red to energize, blue for calmness, indigo to reduce obsessions, violet for relaxation, and white for meditation and sleep. Whatever color you choose, color breathing is a way to restore energy and balance your chakras on the spot.

Stretch to Your Heart's (and Other Chakras') Content

Here are a few stretching exercises that can help keep both your body and chakras fit. These simple techniques not only help to balance the indicated chakras, but warm up and tone muscles as well. Remember, only stretch as far as you are comfortable. Take it at your own pace. What may appear as ordinary stretching offers extraordinary results—and your gym partner will never suspect.

• **Pelvic Tilt (Chakra 1)**
The pelvic tilt requires that you lie flat on the floor on a rug, mat, or blanket and put your feet up on a chair. Take a couple of deep breaths. Make sure your neck is relaxed. Use a neck roll or towel if needed. Begin by lifting your tailbone slowly and precisely from the floor, releasing all tension in your lower back. Continue lifting your hips off the floor vertebra by vertebra, rising no higher than three to four inches off the ground. Remember, you are not in a limbo contest. This movement should be performed gently and without forced resistance. After one breath, lower your hips slowly to the ground, vertebra by vertebra. Notice the flow of warm energy up your spine. Repeat six times.

• **Pelvic Rock (Chakra 2)**
Stand with your feet shoulder distance apart and parallel, your knees slightly bent. Rock your pelvis from front to back. Repeat several times. Now, with your hands on your hips, rotate your pelvis, creating small circles first clockwise and then counterclockwise. Repeat several times.

- **Twists (Chakra 3)**

Sit in a cross-legged position. Reach upward with your hands and then, bending your elbows, grasp your shoulders from above with your fingers resting on your front and your thumbs on your back. Take a deep breath and twist to the right; exhale and twist to the left. Make sure your shoulders are back and your spine is erect but not rigid. For several minutes, continue twisting slowly with each breath. Rest for a moment and then repeat the entire exercise while kneeling.

- **Modified Dog Pose (Chakra 4)**

The modified dog pose is designed to lengthen the spine as well as open the entire front of the body. Begin by standing in front of a wall about one leg length away with feet placed hip distance apart. Slowly bend at the hips until your pelvis and legs are at a ninety-degree angle. Reach out and place your hands on the wall directly in front of you, shoulder height from the floor. Press your hands firmly into the wall, making sure your arms are straight in order to achieve a full stretch from your hands to your hips. Walk your feet back until you reach the maximum stretch in your spine. You should feel completely extended, but not hyperextended. Remember, only stretch within your comfort zone. Hold for several moments or as long as you'd like and feel your body open from both the front and the back. When you are ready to end the pose, walk toward the wall and then release your arms.

- **Head and Neck Stretches (Chakra 5)**

The object of this exercise is to be gentle and relaxed. We are not doing army calisthenics. Done correctly, this exercise can soften the neck and shoulder area as well as release tension in the face. By using soft and slow, purposeful movements, the neck area can recover its freedom and grace. Begin sitting cross-legged on the floor, your upper back and torso in a balanced and comfortable position. Exhaling completely, gently drop your head until your right ear is over your right shoulder, keeping all tension out of your right shoulder area. After a few breaths, return your head to center. Then drop your head until your left ear is positioned over your left shoulder. Finish by returning your head to center again. Repeat in all directions, imagining that you are cutting a pie into six even wedges. Extend forward next, return to center, and then perform the opposite or backward stretch. Remember to return to center after each stretch. Repeat in each direction. Adding sound to this exercise helps open the throat chakra. After completing the first rotation, sing a single vowel sound and feel the front of your throat open.

- **Raising Your Eyebrows (Chakra 6)**

This simple exercise is great for releasing tension in your forehead and for stimulating the sixth chakra. In a sitting or standing position, raise your eyebrows repeatedly, using those forehead muscles that are often forgotten. Notice the stimulation, warmth, and relaxation that follow this exercise.

- **Crowning Your Head (Chakra 7)**

Massage the crown of your head briskly with the tips of your fingers for a few minutes and end by gently rubbing in a clockwise motion. Notice the increased energy flow you have stimulated in your scalp area.

Stretch for chakra fitness. Vibrate your body in the key of balance. Ground yourself in the pulsations of Mother Earth. Give your chakras a tune-up and glide beautifully through another day.

Chapter 9

Angels, Devas, and Spirits of the Earth

Heavenly and
Earthly Assistants

WHEN I WAS NINETEEN years old I had an encounter with an angel. Late one afternoon, I drove to a post office in a high-crime area with my nine-month-old baby to post an urgent package. After using the last of my money to ship the package, I returned to my car to find that I had a flat tire and no spare to change it. Beside my car stood a stately, well-dressed man, gentle in nature, with an almost ethereal quality about his appearance. He insisted that my child and I remain locked safely in my car while he removed the tire and took it to a garage for repair. When he returned, he put the tire back on, refusing any offers to repay him, and then after a hug watched me safely depart from the area. As I drove away, I looked back to find he was gone as if he had vanished into thin air.

Angels Here and Now

Who are these winged creatures that have taken the country by storm? A Gallup poll shows roughly 72 percent of adults in America believe in the existence of angels. In fact, one out of seven has had an encounter with an angel or a similar super-natural experience. Angel mania consumes the country. There are swarms of angel books, angel stores, angel newsletters, angel seminars, angel ornaments for the dashboard, and even an angel postage stamp. Cherub pins hitch rides on legions of lapels and angel cards hail heavenly messages for the day. These celestial spirits are appearing in local newspaper articles, are the subject of national talk shows, and have made the cover of *Time* magazine. Hollywood continues to launch programs featuring angels with overwhelming success. Even the scientific community is buzzing about these winged protectors. At a seminar hosted in my hometown, cosmonauts and astronauts came together to share their experiences while in space. A surprising common denominator arose during this conference—their stories of encounters with angelic beings. Today's world, with its striving for technological knowledge, has left our spiritual aspirations by the wayside. People are hungry for information and communication with all types of angels and other guardian spirits.

Where Do Angels Come From?

The word *angel* has many roots. The Greek word *angelos* means "messenger." In Hebrew, *aggelos* means "the one sent." According to Christian theology, angels were created separately, operating as an ethereal link between God and humans. Another race of intelligent beings, they are far more evolved than the human being. Although these spirits are not of the physical world, they sometimes manifest in human form whenever need arises, leaving when the job is done. Angels appear in more than half of the books of the Bible, but they are not linked exclusively to Christianity. All the major religions of the world include celestial beings and stories of their intervention. In fact, stories of winged or flying spirits have appeared in the cultures and legends of almost every civilization. In ancient mythology, angels were reported to have the power to turn planets, ignite stars, and nurture the plant and animal kingdoms, inspiring all of creation. Mohammed's teachings speak of these beings emerging from clear, radiant gems. Even people who don't believe in organized religion are calling for angelic and otherworldly assistance.

Regardless of their origin, these celestial beings are our lightning rods, our connection with heavenly realms. In all beliefs, they are beings that answer to a higher power and symbolize unconditional love.

What Is an Angel's Job?

Imagine there's a top Fortune 500 firm running the operation of the divine realms of heaven. Angels have their own specialty and mission statement: We bring heaven to your lives. There are permanent departments with offices for archangels, guardian angels, recording angels, and messenger angels. Then, there are all-occasion angels, Johnny-on-the-spot types, available twenty-four hours a day for all types of services. There are angels called in for specific jobs, such as planning angels, rescuers, fun executives, problem solvers, test takers, culinary masters, and stand-up comics. Whatever office they come from, their intentions are the same. They are here to help ease humans' journey from ordinary reality to spiritual life, to transform our ordinary into the extraordinary. They relay messages from higher-ups, instill ideas, and help us to understand our own inner beauty. They do not interfere with our free will, but if we want their help, they stand ready without judgment, malice, or prejudice. They are our hot line to heaven and their services are free. And in all life's situations, they remind us to laugh and take things lightly.

Touched by Spirit

How do you know if you have been touched by spirit? In some cases, you may feel as if you were struck by a bolt of lightning with direct and intimate contact. Unlikely helpers may pull you from a burning building or orchestrate an unexplainable rescue, subsequently leaving without a trace. Other times they may emerge as a mist or fog that slowly seeps into your consciousness, whispering messages that guide you along the way. Or perhaps, they appear as a series of coincidences that cannot be dismissed. To a few, they come as the vision of an angelic spirit in form, miraculously revealed. And what happens after you have had a spiritual or mystical experience? You may well feel confused and experience denial, along with incredible joy. You return to everyday life and find that nothing is quite the same, and that everything has been touched by your reconnection to love.

In the following section, we explore many ways to communicate with angels and other spirits. Through exploration of nature, we investigate the magical world of the nature spirits and the concept of the Native Americans' spirits of the earth. Whatever way we choose, opening our lives up to these wondrous realms will uplift our spirits and send our gaze to heavenly skies.

Exercising with Angels

Calling All Angels

Calling in help from the angels, the celestial realm that is closest to humans, has been used by people for thousands of years. Specific angels are often called upon for specific needs. And for good reason. There are angels for each season, for each month, for each day of the week, and for each of the directions. There are angel specialists for just about everything. Included is a list of just a few angels and the realms they rule. After identifying the task or issue you want to pray for, sit quietly and call the angel's name three times to invoke this celestial being. Tune in to the angel's loving energy and notice the evidence of celestial assistance as it weaves through your life.

- Archangel Michael both shields us and engages in battles on our behalf. This angel is the warrior angel who carries a sword and cuts through to the clear discernment of a situation. When you need protection or clarity, call on Michael.
- Archangel Raphael rules all of the healing arts. When you are in need of physical healing for yourself or want to assist others, call on Raphael to help.
- Archangel Gabriel is the bearer of God's secret messages and prophecy and can help us with intuition. His name literally translates as "he who brings hope." Praying to Gabriel can offer both hope and nurturing.
- Archangel Uriel is the angel of justice seen with the scales in hand. This angel also holds the key to ancient knowledge. When you seek justice or when you have been unjustly accused, pray to Uriel.
- Archangel Zadkiel is the angel of benevolence and mercy. Zadkiel guards over the spiritual development of humans and rules prayer. When you are in need of gentle comfort or wish to empower your prayers, call on Zadkiel.
- Archangel Barachiel is the guardian and provider for children. This angel is also connected with prosperity and abundance. Call on Barachiel to protect children or when you want to bring in abundance.
- Archangel Chammuel has dominion over many powers and natural forces and helps to accomplish goals. Call on Chammuel to assist in finishing a task or to accomplish a daunting objective.

- Archangel Zophkiel is the ruler of spirit guides. Zophkiel can help us when we are in need of additional guidance.

Other angels you may want to call on:

- Yehudia is a tender and loving guide to those who are making the transition to death. Prayers to Yehudia can help assist a soul's passage to the afterlife.
- Kadmiel guides new souls to earth and is a protector of new mothers. Kadmiel is often called on during pregnancy and childbirth.
- Haniel rules over affection, love, and ability to see beauty. Prayers to Haniel can assist in fostering harmony in friendships and social situations.

These are a few of the angels that you may want to invoke. You can call on thousands of others. After calling in your angel, offer your prayers and see what magic unfolds.

Guardian Angel

Guardian angels are one of the best-known and most frequently prayed-to realms of angels. It is believed that an angel is placed at your side at birth and stays with you until your last breath. This angel is truly a great ally and is ready to help guide you at the least provocation. This meditation exercise offers you a way to sit quietly with and gather guidance from the angel(s) that surround(s) you always.

Find a peaceful room where you feel at ease. You can make it more beautiful by adding flowers, candles, crystals, or any objects that are sacred to you. Burning your favorite incense will help set the mood. Remember, when reading this script for others or recording it for yourself, wait twenty to thirty seconds at each ellipsis (…) and wait one minute or longer at each "(Pause)."

Guardian Angel Meditation Script

Begin by sitting or lying in a comfortable position. Take several full, deep breaths. Inhale life-giving breath deeply … exhale fully, allowing your body to relax and your mind to release all tensions and worries. (Pause) Now, closing your eyes, begin to see a brilliant light above you. Reaching upward, open your arms to receive this light. (Pause) As the light moves toward you, you begin to see a light-filled form, an angel emerging from the light … Know that this is your guardian angel. As the glow of this being surrounds you, embrace your angel, knowing that this being has been your lifelong companion, guide, and protector … Basking in this warm light, feel loved and cherished. (Pause)

Imagine now that your guardian angel stands in front of you and with a luminous feather touches your heart with a gentle stroke … A point of light radiates and expands, filling your heart and then your entire body. (Pause)

Notice that your angel is beckoning you to an emerald-green path that stretches before you … Walking with your angel, you come upon a crystal bridge. Turning toward you, your angel informs you that by crossing this bridge you will enter into a realm different from your own, a realm of angels. You cross this bridge with your angel at your side. (Pause) Your angel leads you to a beautifully carved stone bench in a garden filled with blossoming trees, the fragrance of wildflowers, a musical stream, and birds of all colors singing … You know instantly that this is a healing garden, a safe and peaceful place. You feel totally at ease. (Pause)

Remembering that this angel is a great ally, share something that is troubling you or ask for some needed advice. Talk with your angel and confide all of your thoughts and feelings about your life or present situation … If, when your angel responds, you do not understand what the angel is telling you, ask for this information to be shown to you in a different way. Or ask to be taken to a specific teacher or guide for the information you seek. Take all the time you need. (Pause)

When you feel that your time with your guardian angel is coming to a close, thank this being for the experience and for the information you have received ... Crossing back over the bridge, follow the path back to the present ... Know that your angel is always with you, and you may return for guidance whenever you like ... When you are ready, open your eyes.

The Wings of Angels

Here's a visualization that can help in a hurry when you're feeling especially vulnerable and in need of extra protection. Whether you are at work, in a crowded room, or on a subway traveling home, imagine that your entire being, including your head and feet, is enfolded in a circle of angels' wings. Feel the feathery texture of the wings and the warmth of the golden light that surrounds you. Know that you are bathed in love and protection. Return to your environment feeling watched over and secure.

Nature Spirits

The word *angel* is a general term referring to all celestial beings. Nature spirits are the part of the angel kingdom that are expressed through the four elements: earth, air, fire, water. The nature spirits connected with the earth are frequently referred to as gnomes. They are the guardians of the rocks, gems, metals and hidden treasures, trees, and plants. The water spirits called the undines are connected with lakes, fountains, rivers, streams, even the humidity in the air, and are associated with stormy emotions. The excitable sylphs are the spirits of the air and are as volatile and changeable as the wind. The fire spirits, the salamanders, are lizard-like in shape and are connected with a fiery temper akin with all fire. In Africa we see these nature spirits as the *yowahoos.* In the Buddhist tradition, they are the *dakinis.* The Hebrews call these spirits the *shedin* and to the Persians they are the *devs.*

The wee people have been woven into the fabric of myths, fairy tales, and agricultural practices throughout the ages. Years ago, ashes from sacred fires, along with soil from mountain-tops, were spread in the newly planted fields. Offerings of fruits from the previous year's harvest, bread, cheese, and milk consecrated the soil. Whiskey, "the water of life," was poured over all farming equipment, blessing it for the new season. Hilltop fires were lit to mirror the warmth and love of the great earth mother. All of these were offered to the wee people, the nature spirits that oversaw the success of each harvest. Some of these practices are still performed today.

Still, who are these peculiar beings? Do they really exist or are they just stories from another time? Some of the greatest minds of the world—Socrates, Plato, Paracelsus—believed in the existence of fairies and nature spirits and claimed that just as humans are made of body, mind, and spirit, the plant and mineral worlds are also composed of these elements. They and others held that just as visible nature is inhabited by countless varieties of familiar creatures, the invisible world of nature is populated by beings, nature spirits living in realms of their own. Humanoid in form, these beings have the ability to move at great speed, remaining undetected by the unevolved senses of humans. These nature spirits are the animating force, the soul, of the plant and mineral kingdoms.

Our children know these beings well as Tinker Bell, Snow White's Seven Dwarfs, Ariel the mermaid, the silkies in *The Secret Life of Roan Inish,* and the elves and dwarfs in *The Lord of the Rings,* to name just a few. As adults, they live in our hearts as symbols of luck, joy, magic, mischief, and temptation, bursting forth with the first hint of spring and making their homes in the dew-covered forests and fields of flowers everywhere. On your next outing in the woods, if you are especially quiet and sit as still as a statue, you may be lucky enough to catch a leprechaun and earn a wish.

Gardening with the Devas

In close kinship with the angels are the *devas*, who work with the plants, animals, and minerals. The word *deva* is a Sanskrit word meaning "intelligent agent."

Ask for assistance from the wee people the next time you plant your vegetable or flower garden. They are longing for an invitation. First, find the focal point, heart, or center of your garden. This probably won't be the geographic center. Use your intuition to *feel* the spot or ask the little people for help, and then sit in your garden and listen for the response. When you find the center, place an offering there. It can be a crystal, an elfin statue acknowledging the land elementals, or a fountain honoring the water spirits or sylphs. Or plant a sacred plant such as artemisia (sage), holly, hollyhocks, or corn. Then watch your garden bloom. You may even want to create an area where you can sit quietly to commune with the fairies. Once the plants are in full bloom, take time to tune in to the energy that surrounds them, their shimmering aura. Maybe if you're lucky and very, very quiet, you will actually see a nature spirit, much to the envy of your neighbors.

Walking in the Woods

Next time you take a walk in the forest, make it a reverent one. Native Americans believe the earth is our mother and the surface of the earth is her face. Walk softly and make each footstep a gentle kiss. While you are in this quiet, respectful place, try to see in your peripheral vision the nature spirits that inhabit this kingdom. Sit quietly on a rock or with your back against the trunk of your favorite tree, tune in to the abundance and generosity of this unconditional planet, and wait. If you don't catch a glimpse, don't despair. They are probably hiding nearby curiously watching you.

Gifts for Our Earth Mother

Another way to relate to nature spirits is through the practices and beliefs of our own indigenous people. Many Native Americans have an intimate and sacred relationship with a host of beings, similar to the relationship other cultures have with angels. They believe that every tree, rock, river, mountain, and creature that shares this earth and sky has spirit. These spirits are considered loving ancestors. They are often called upon for assistance and intervention and are invoked for guidance.

When you are enjoying the many gifts that Mother Earth has given us, why not give something back? On your next outing, tune in to your surroundings and see what may need tending. You may want to pick up a few pieces of litter or help maintain the path you are on with a few rocks. The idea is not to get overwhelmed if the area needs more attention than you can possibly give it. Every little bit helps. Or bring with you an offering of bird seed and a homemade suet cake for your feathered counterparts, sugar for the ants, and some of your drinking water for a thirsty tree. Offerings such as cornmeal, tobacco, or a package of wildflower seeds for the little people can acknowledge and nourish them in their path of service. Our intent to feed these beings and heal the earth feeds us too. As you are leaving trails of offerings behind, remember that Johnny Appleseed got his start this way.

Mitakuye Oyasin ("All Our Relations")

The Native American culture considers the earth as the source of life, not just a natural resource. In fact, Native Americans believe that we are related to every spirit on this planet, including the insects, the animals, the fish, and the mineral and plant kingdoms. Here's an exercise that uses the phrase *Mitakuye Oyasin* ("all our relations") that allows you to connect with these spirits. Through this connection we can learn to live a more harmonious life with our mother, the earth, and all her inhabitants.

The next time you are out in nature, take a moment to sit quietly and closely observe the world around you. Notice the ants building a nearby home, a bee buzzing near your ear, the plants that sway in the wind around you, the birds in the sky, the sky above you, and the ground you rest on. Notice everything in your environment and acknowledge that we are all interdependent. We are all related in one big family, in one circle of life. Then send a blessing to all that surrounds you by saying *Mitakuye Oyasin* (pronounced mee-tak-wee-ay oy-ah-sin). Enjoy the beauty in knowing that you are truly an intricate part of the incredible web of life that surrounds you.

The Seventh Generation

Another understanding of the Native Americans is that every action and decision we make today affects the children born seven generations from now. This simple awareness gives us the opportunity to reflect on all our actions and thoughts and offer them as a blessing to our future generations.

Here are some suggestions for change that can have a powerful impact on the seventh generation. Recycling our rubbish, limiting our use of pesticides and herbicides on our lawns and gardens, cutting down the amount of water we use, using Xeriscape methods for landscaping, growing indigenous plants, working to protect local and national parks, electing ecologically minded government officials, registering with local and national agencies to remove our name from wasteful junk mail lists, planting trees, growing some of our own food, and preserving fertile seeds are a few suggestions. There are many more opportunities to positively affect future generations. When you make your next decision, try looking forward to how it will influence the lives of the seventh generation. Enjoying conscious and harmonious living today will help create the same for the world of tomorrow.

Making a difficult decision? Try communing with the angels for advice. Lost and disconnected from the world around you? Take a walk in the forest and play hide-and-seek with the *devas*. Feeling powerless? Connect with the wondrous circle of life. Whatever you are in need of, calling all angels and other guardians will lift your tired spirit and send you soaring every time.

Chapter 10

Prayer and Positive Thoughts

Accentuate the Positive, Eliminate the Negative

ABOUT TEN YEARS AGO, I witnessed an astonishing miracle. During a weekend workshop I cofacilitated, I met a fifty-year-old woman suffering from a rare physical disease. A tumor fully encased her heart. She was told by her doctors that her condition was inoperable and there was absolutely nothing they could do to help her. It so incapacitated her that she could not walk around the block. During the workshop, she recognized that she had been deeply hurt throughout her life, and in a way had chosen to protect her heart by completely confining it. We administered hands-on energy work throughout the weekend and invited all the participants to pray for a healing to take place. She was surrounded by positive affirmations, group prayers, and love. A couple of weeks later, she returned to her doctor, who told her with some amazement that her tumor was dissipating. Within six weeks after the workshop, the tumor had totally disappeared. Four months later, she led a group of close friends on a hike to the bottom of the Grand Canyon and back up again.

A Positive Thought a Day

"Unbelievable!" you may think, yet the power of our thoughts is astounding. Recent medical research has proven that what we think profoundly affects our physical and psychological health. Positive thinking such as prayer has been found to offer the same biochemical response as deep relaxation and meditation. By stimulating the limbic brain, prayer and positive thinking can reduce the production of "stress hormones," lower blood pressure, and relax the heart and other bodily functions while boosting the immune system.

Other research indicates that prayers and other positive thinking can actually reduce or eliminate the need for pain medication. Pain is a complex mixture of emotional and physical processes. Fostering a positive outlook calms the emotions, boosting the body's natural healing ability. By contrast, negative thinking can actually release chemicals that increase the pain a patient feels. Research has shown that negative thinking in HIV patients supports a rapid decline in infection-fighting T cells.

A *Time* magazine poll found that 82 percent of Americans are convinced of the potent healing power of prayer and positive thinking. Since 60 percent of all doctor's visits are due to a mind-body stress-related disease, medical science is looking for some new answers. Medical schools across the nation are offering alternative courses to help future doctors take a more spiritual, mind-body approach to medical care.

What You Think

According to the Theosophical Society, thoughts, although invisible, have a physical form or shape. Likened to a radio or television wave, thoughts travel through the airways, vibrating at a certain level and even radiating a color. This color is often associated with the emotion the sender attaches to the thought. Thoughts sent out from one person toward another can actually alter the auric field of the receiver and influence him or her. How often do we think of someone and suddenly they telephone us? Or feel a sudden sadness just before a close relative or friend calls us with bad news? This illustrates our ability to receive thought forms. We have all experienced this type of perception in our everyday lives. The more concentrated, clear, and directed the thought or thought form, the stronger the effect.

Positive thought forms such as prayer, positive affirmations, and blessings can bring about incredible healing and dynamic change in our lives. Energized positive thought forms have been recorded by Kirlian photography and clairvoyants alike. These thought forms appear as an additional band of protection and healing in the aura of the recipient. The sender also benefits. Sending benefic thought forms blesses the aura of the sender with the same vibration.

By contrast, when negative thoughts are directed toward a person or environment, that energy field is adversely affected. The folklore of all cultures describes this phenomenon as a "curse" or "hex." We have all experienced this at some time in our lives in situations with an angry boss, a jealous coworker, a hurt lover, or a worried parent. Anger, jealousy, fear, worry, or other negative thought forms directed toward another person can result in debris that attaches to the auric field, creating static and adversely influencing everything around that person. You may experience this after walking into the home of people who have just waged a major fight. Thus the adage "tension so thick you can cut it with a knife." Likewise, if you are the sender, negative thought forms will pollute your aura and environment as well.

Researching the Power of Prayer

Research has shown that positive thought forms, especially prayer and blessing, have significant quantitative results. This was proven in a famous test conducted by a physician who was analyzing the germination rate of seeds. In the test, rye seeds were planted in vermiculite in a shallow container and separated by a string that divided the flat into two sections. Side A became the control group and side B the test group. After the seeds were sown, those on side B were prayed for while the seeds on side A were not. At the end of the experiment, side B sprouted significantly more rye shoots than side A. This test was repeated many times by many practitioners including subjects such as yeast, pacemaker cells, mice, red blood cells, and many others resulting in the same conclusion: the effect of prayer and positive thought on living organisms is substantial, quantifiable, and reproducible.

Further tests were conducted, stressing the environment by adding saltwater to the vermiculite. The results showed that the saltier the water-vermiculite solution, the higher the rate of germination of side B plants. This indicates that prayer or positive thoughts work best when the organism is under stress. In fact, the more stressed the environment, the more effective the use of prayer and positive thinking.

Another experiment was conducted with soybean seeds planted in four containers: container A held the control group, which was not prayed for; containers B and C held seeds that were prayed for for the same amount of time; and container D held seeds that were prayed for twice as long as B and C. The doubly blessed container D resulted in exactly twice the seed germination of containers B and C, suggesting that the amount of prayer was directly proportionate to the results. Another study examined the type of prayers and their potency. The simple "Thy will be done" prayer was found to be more effective than prayers asking for specific results.

Since then, many experiments using prayer and positive thinking have been conducted with human participants. In a double-blind study conducted with human cardiac patients, one-half of 393 cardiac patients were prayed for while the control group was not. The group of patients who were prayed for did remarkably better than the control group, who required five times more antibiotics and a significantly longer time for rehabilitation. A Duke University study involving cardiac patients measured the recovery rate of a control group compared to groups that received additional treatments of touch therapy, lessons in guided imagery, relaxation training, or prayers without their knowledge. Although all of these groups showed a significant reduction in complications when compared to the control group, the prayed-for group achieved the lowest complication rate of all.

A medical study conducted with advanced AIDS patients discovered prayer positively influenced overall health. One group of AIDS patients received an hour of prayer six days a week while a control group did not. After ten weeks, the group that was prayed for was found to be notably healthier than the control group.

Another study examined the effect of prayer on the heart by testing a group that recited the rosary while another used a yoga mantra. After a short time, both groups achieved a respiratory rate of six breaths per minute, which synchronizes with cardiovascular rhythms that have a six-per-minute cycle, positively affecting heart function.

In other studies, patients who were prayed for required 29 percent fewer visits to the doctor, developed 83 percent fewer illnesses, and spent 85 percent less time in the hospital than the control group. More and more medical journals and mainstream media report that prayer and positive thinking increase the healing rate of wounds during rehabilitation, and patients often make a remarkable comeback without medical intervention.

Planting the Seeds

It is time now to review the important lessons of the power of thought, prayers, and how we participate in our own healing or demise. The intention of this book is to help each of us become a healthier human being and allow our thoughts, through personal healing, to continue in a positive way. The following exercises offer additional ways to launch our prayers and blessings, cleanse our aura, and polish our armor while dealing with everyday life. And better yet, these exercises offer ways to transcend it all with love and gratitude in our hearts. Remember, you reap what you sow. So plant the seeds of love and kindness and your life will be filled with gardens of joy.

Exercises with Prayer and Positive Thinking

Counting Your Blessings

Our challenge as human beings is to enjoy life to the fullest. It does not mean that we won't be tested along the way. On the contrary, life is sometimes unpleasant, hard, full of tasks that require us to stretch beyond our comfort zones and boundaries. Living in joy requires a present-time appreciation that recognizes each moment as a gift. Each day our life offers us the opportunity to enjoy the simplest blessings—from a bird singing outside our window to the gentle breathing that continues to offer us life for another day. Pulling our minds away from the negative takes a shift in conscious awareness to recognize the precious life we lead and be grateful for it. Here's an exercise that can remind us of all we have to be thankful for.

Let your mind roam and bring your attention to things and/or persons that enrich your life but that you often overlook. Write a list of all the things you are grateful for. You might start with some basics like the water you drink, the tree outside your window, the window itself, the air you breathe. Go on and on. Fill up at least one side of a page with things or relationships you now see as gifts. After you are done making the list, take a minute to say thank you to each item mentioned. You'll be uplifted by this prayer of gratitude and this new appreciation for the gifts that surround you.

Bringing in the Light

This is another exercise designed to burn away all the negative thought forms that have been sent to you or that you have sent to others. It is a great exercise to do at the conclusion of a hectic day.

Begin by finding a quiet room where there will be no distractions. Burn your favorite incense or sage or set out a bowl of saltwater to act as a cleansing and protecting agent. Place a white candle on a table or desk. Then light the candle and for five minutes stare into the flame, purging your mind of any thoughts. After you have concentrated on the flame for five minutes, close your eyes, continuing to see the flame in your mind. Now ask that all the negative thoughts and feelings that plague you be consumed by this flame. Visualize these thought forms burning one by one in the light of the fire, cleansing away all of the unhappiness and negativity you have been feeling. When you are finished, open your eyes and return to a better world.

Showering Blessings

The Latin root of *bless* is *benedicia,* which means "calling a thing good." When we send out blessings to another, we are in essence recognizing the good in the receiver. When we bless someone or something, we send it an inherent message, a wish for its continued existence and enhanced well-being.

Children respond to this concept beautifully. Sprinkle your children or grandchildren with positive encouragement and watch them blossom before your eyes. The act of blessing allows life force to flow outward to a receiver, returning to you in a continual current.

Take a couple of minutes each day to send out blessings to everyone and everything in your environment. Find the positive in everything you see. You might begin with yourself by saying, "I am a loving person." Then bless the plants in your house, even if they are a little wilted: "You are the most beautiful plants in this house and I thank you for the oxygen you give me." With the simple act of blessing, by recognizing the good in a person or thing, we can bring out the best in what we bless and energize it with life force. Bless three people a day even if you don't see eye to eye. Remember, Christ said, "Bless your enemies." Take the opportunity to send blessings to all around you when you are stuck in traffic or in a long line at the grocery store. *Warning:* This action can become habit-forming. You may suddenly find yourself blessing auditors, lawyers, and referees! You won't believe how good it will make you feel.

White Light Ovoid

There may be times when you feel you need a little help clearing chaos and static from daily events, whether it is an argument with your boss, a traffic jam, or the ominous and depressing evening news. This visualization can give protection as well as create an inner sanctuary for you to return to whenever you need it.

Begin by visualizing your aura as an egg-shaped magnetic field extending beneath your feet and above your head. Imagine that within this ovoid, a surging violet light enters, beginning at your feet and swirling up from your feet through your lower torso, upper torso, then rising above the top of your head, cleansing you of any negativity. Now, fill the ovoid with a soft white light emanating from your heart. Allow it to expand, illuminating and energizing your body, mind, and spirit. Feel a sense of wholeness and love filling this ovoid. Let thoughts of protection and expansion replace your feelings of vulnerability and permeability. Congratulations! You have created a protective shield to cleanse away the day's negative events and intrusive outside forces.

Smudging

A Native American tradition for cleansing negative energy is called "smudging" or "smoking." You need to first acquire a smudge stick made of dried sage and cedar or sweet grass. You can find these inexpensive bundles at most new age bookstores, health food stores, or even farmer's markets. Or you may pick the herbs yourself while on a nature walk and dry them thoroughly. Place the dried herbs in a fireproof vessel to be used only for this procedure, or hold a smudge stick and light it. After the initial flame, the herbs will smoke slowly, continuously, like tobacco. Relight if necessary. To cleanse your environment, use a large feather or handheld fan to spread the smoke around the room. Starting at the easternmost spot, move in a sunrise or clockwise direction around the room. Some Native American traditions require a door or window be left ajar to release negative energy. A similar process can be used to cleanse your auric field. Using the same lighted materials and a fan or your hand, disperse smoke around your body from head to toe. To complete the offering, you can add a small amount of cornmeal to the vessel as a thank-you.

Becoming a Star

When you feel in danger of a psychic attack, such as anger, jealousy, or envy directed at you, or you have picked up "bad vibes" from a certain environment, first cleanse yourself mentally and then imagine that you are encased by a luminescent, five-pointed star. Begin by standing with your legs hip distance apart and arms outstretched. In your mind, draw a star around you, beginning with a point of light at the pinnacle or top of the star surrounding your head. Then see the star extending over your right arm, forming the right point, and then to your left arm. Finally, draw the last two points encasing your legs. Feel the sparkling star around you. By mentally drawing a protective star, you are creating a positive force field that is a very powerful and effective tool of protection.

Checking In

We're not only influenced by thought forms that are sent to us but also by the thoughts we send out. Try this: Before you go to sleep at night, spend five minutes reviewing the day's events. Pick a particular scene that is clear in your mind and examine the feelings, thoughts, and behavior you experienced during this incident, as if you were watching a movie. Observe this scene as an outsider, without judgment, and ask yourself these questions: "Was I reacting from pain, anger, mistrust, or fear?" "How was my ego entangled in the action?" Now, take a minute and ask that any negative thoughts and feelings you have sent out during that day be dissolved. Feel the inner balance as it is restored again.

Launch Your Blessings

Relax on the floor or sit in a comfortable chair. Take a few deep breaths. Bring your attention to the top of your head, or crown chakra, and imagine above your head a beam of golden light filled with love and healing energies. Feel the beam penetrate your crown, filling your head and traveling down to your heart chakra. Allow this light, the energy of unconditional love, to surround your heart and fill your aura. Feel it build until your whole body is tingling with it. Give yourself permission to feel as happy as you possibly can. When you feel totally energized, launch these good feelings and thoughts toward someone or something.

A Circle for Earth Healing

Gathering together to pray or to ask for blessings can greatly amplify the power of the prayer. Try this visualization at your next party, family gathering, or group meeting. You or another willing participant can lead the group. If you would like to fully join in, record the narration before your company arrives. This exercise is guaranteed to raise the roof off an otherwise ordinary event. The ellipses (…) indicate a brief pause; "(Pause)" indicates one minute or longer.

Group Leader's Script

From a sitting or standing position, form a circle, holding hands. Silently, call in your guardian angel, spiritual guide, god or goddess, or elements of nature that you are strongly connected with and feel protected and loved by … As you visualize the presence behind you, focus on your heart area and see a sphere of golden light emanating from there … Now send this energy to the person on your right, moving it from your heart to your right shoulder, down your arm, and to your right hand. At the same time, receive this loving energy from the person to your left. Feel the circle vibrate with energy waves of love. (Pause)

Next, picture this benevolent presence behind you … See your guide joining hands with the other beings present, forming another circle, completing an outward ring of protection and love. (Pause)

Now visualize an image of our planet, Mother Earth, and project this image into the center of the circle, seeing it rotate gently in space ... Focus on the planet, seeing in great detail all of its waters—oceans, seas, rivers, streams, and lakes ... As you tune in to these areas, see them as being pure, clear, healthy, and supporting all their aquatic inhabitants beautifully. Focus beneath the surface of the water and take a minute to imagine the playful movement of the fish, plant life, sea turtles, crustaceans, whales, dolphins, and other aquatic creatures as they bask in this healthy environment ... Shining the golden loving light from your heart chakra toward the waters, send blessings and heartfelt prayers asking that these waters be continually renewed. Ask your guides to direct these prayers to the waters of our planet. (Pause)

Next, focus on the landmasses of our planet and see the deep, dark richness of the soil and the lush green of the tropical forest ... Picture the land purged of toxicity and the forest healed. See all the animals of the plains, mountains, deserts, and forests living in perfect harmony in this healthy environment ... Shine loving light from your heart chakra, surrounding these lands with blessings and prayers that perfect healing will take place. Ask your guides to amplify the energy of these prayers. (Pause)

Now, create a picture of earth's atmosphere in your mind. See blue skies, white puffy clouds, the winged beings, and crystal-clear air surrounding our planet, enveloping it in perfect harmony ... Breathe this clean air in and out, through your nostrils, sending this image of healthy air to the center of the circle ... Again, send out blessings and love to the air that surrounds you and pray for a healthy atmosphere to be restored ... Ask your guides to direct your wishes to the air that surrounds us ... Ask also that they assist in making all of your visions reality. Direct the loving light of your heart chakra to the center image of a healthy and perfect world. (Pause)

Now, release your hands and bring them to your heart, returning the loving energy created in the circle to yourself … Feel your guide embrace you in love … Experience gratitude for all that have participated in this gathering—your guide, yourself, the people in the circle, and Mother Earth. (Pause) When you are ready, allow your consciousness to return to the room and open your eyes.

Do a candle meditation and burn away the negativity of the day. Draw a shimmering star around your body and encase yourself in its protection. Say a prayer for a friend or stranger and launch it. At your next party, visualize a perfect planet and send healing energies to Mother Earth. Get hooked on the positive and shower your blessings all around you for a better life … a better world.

Bibliography

Chapter 1: Sound Therapy

Campbell, Don G. *The Roar of Silence*. IL: Theosophical Publishing House, 1989.

Chopra, Deepak. *Magical Mind, Magical Body*. IL: Nightingale-Conan, 1990. Audioassette.

Dodd, Vickie. "Sound as a Tool for Transformation." *Halo* (winter 1989), pp. 24–27.

Dodd, Vickie. *Tuning the Blues to Gold: Soundprints*. CO: Woven-Word Press, 1999.

Gardner, Kay. *Sounding the Inner Landscape: Music as Medicine*. ME: Caduceus Publications, 1990.

Halpern, Steven. *Sound Health: The Music and Sounds That Make Us Whole*. NY: Harper and Row, 1985.

Hamel, Peter Michael. *Through Music to the Self*. MA: Shambhala Publications, 1979.

Jenny, Hans. *Cymatics*. Switzerland: Basilius Press, 1974.

Jenny, Hans. *Cymatics*. MA: Macromedia, 1986. Videotape.

Judith, Anodea. *Wheels of Life: A User's Guide to the Chakras*. MN: Llewellyn Publications, 1987.

Khalsa, Dharma Singh, and Cameron Stauth. *Meditation as Medicine: Activate the Power of Your Natural Healing Force*. NY: Pocket Books, 2001.

Kittelson, Mary Lynn. *Sounding the Soul: The Art of Listening*. Switzerland: Daimon, 1996.

Mayo Foundation for Medical Education and Research. "Mayo Clinic Health Letter." *Muscle and Fitness* 55 (October 1994), p. 56.

McGregor, John C. *Southwestern Archaeology*. NY: John Wiley, 1941.

Pert, Candace B. *Molecules of Emotion: Why You Feel the Way You Feel*. NY: Scribner, 1997.

Solomont, Elide M. *You Are Who You Hate: The Alchemy of Dissonance.* NY: Vantage Press, 1995.

Sung, B. H., O. Roussanov, M. Nagvbandi, and L. Golden. "Effectiveness of Various Relaxation Techniques in Lowering Blood Pressure Associated with Mental Stress." *American Journal of Hypertension* 13 (2000), pp. 185A–186A.

Verny, Thomas, with John Kelly. *The Secret Life of the Unborn Child.* NY: Dell Publishing Co., Inc., 1981.

Zucker, Martin. "Music as Medicine Heals." *Let's Live* (April 1994), pp. 62–65.

Chapter 2: Color Therapy

Abramovitz, Melissa. "A SAD State of Mind." *Current Health* 2, 27, no. 5 (January 2001), p. 18.

Anderson, Mary. *Colour Healing, Chromotherapy and How It Works.* NY: Samuel Weiser, 1975.

Birren, Faber. *Color in Your World.* NY: Collier MacMillan, 1978.

Bower, B. "Winter Depression May Heed Hormonal Signal." *Science News* 160, no. 24 (December 2001), p. 374.

Cassata, Carla. "Light, the Ignored Nutrient." *Let's Live* (March 1994), p. 34.

Clark, Linda. *The Ancient Art of Color Therapy.* CT: Devin-Adair Company, 1975.

Hall, Manley P. *The Secret Teachings of All Ages.* CA: Philosophical Research Society, 1988.

Heline, Corinne. *Color and Music in the New Age.* CA: De Vorss and Company, 1982.

Hofer, Stephen. "Color Our World." *Lapidary Journal* 46 (September 1992), pp. 43–102.

Hunt, Roland. *The Seven Keys to Color Healing.* NY: Harper and Row, 1971.

Lewy, A. J., V. K. Bauer, and N. L. Cutler. "Bright Morning Light Reduces Depressive Symptoms in Seasonal Affective Disorder." *Western Journal of Medicine* (November 1999), p. 316.

Mella, Dorothee L. *Color Power.* NM: Domel Artbooks, 1981.

Ouseley, S.G.J. *Colour Meditations.* Essex: L. N. Fowler and Co., 1949.

Potera, Carol. "Nature's Rays Protect the Ovaries." *Natural Health* (December 1995), p. 22.

Thompson, Sharon Elaine. "Color Coordination." *Lapidary Journal* 46 (September 1992), pp. 40–42.

Chapter 3: Aromatherapy

Berwick, Ann. *Holistic Aromatherapy: Balance the Body and the Soul with Essential Oils.* MN: Llewellyn Publications, 1994.

Cooper, Corinne. "Aromatherapy (for Business)." *Inside Business* 4, no. 2 (February 2002), p. 11.

Fischer-Rizzi, Suzanne. *The Complete Aromatherapy Handbook: Essential Oils for Radiant Health.* NY: Sterling, 1990.

Golin, Mark, with Sharon Stocker and Toby Hanlon. "Natural Tranquilizers." *Prevention* (December 1995), p. 65 (10 p.).

Keller, Amy M. "Energy-Boosting Beauty: It's No Hoax." *Redbook* 197, no. 2 (August 2001), p. 110 (4 p.).

Khalsa, Dharma Singh. "Aromatherapy for Alzheimer's." *Yoga Journal* (September/October 2000), p. 44.

Lavabre, Marcel. *Aromatherapy Workbook.* VT: Healing Arts Press, 1990.

Menter, Marcia, ed. "Look Relaxed and Pretty in 10 Minutes or Less." *Redbook* 168, no. 3 (January 1996), p. 82 (5 p.).

Sanabria, Virna. "Aroma Myths: Essential Oils Are Aromatherapy's Truth Serum in the Personal-Care Market." *Global Cosmetic Industry* 169, no. 6 (November 2001), p. 18.

Tisserand, Robert. *Aromatherapy to Heal and Tend the Body.* WI: Lotus Press, 1988.

Tisserand, Robert. *Art of Aromatherapy.* VT: Healing Arts Press, 1977.

Watt, Martin. Lecture on Aromatherapy. Presented by Pat Padilla in Lyons, CO, November 26, 1995.

Chapter 4: Breathing Techniques

Acharya, Pundit. *Breath, Sleep, the Heart, and Life.* CA: The Dawn Horse Press, 1975, p. 177.

A'nanda Ma'rga. *Teaching Asanas: An A'nanda Ma'rga Manual for Teachers.* CA: Amrit Publications, 1973.

Bernardi, Luciano, Cesare Porta, Alessandra Gabutti, Lucia Spicuzza, and Peter Sleight. "Autonomic Neuroscience." *Elsevier Medical Journal* 90, nos. 1–2 (2002), pp. 47–56.

Bernardi, L., P. Sleight, G. Bandinelli, S. Cencetti, L. Fattorini, J. Wdowczyc-Szulc, and A. Lagi. "Effect of Rosary Prayer and Yoga Mantras on Autonomic Cardiovascular Rhythms: Comparative Study." *British Medical Journal* 323 (2001), pp. 1446–1449.

Briggs, Tony. "Breathing Lessons." *Yoga Journal* (November/December 2000), p. 94 (12 p.).

Dodd, Vickie. "Sounding the Respiratory System." Lecture given at the School of Sound and Sacred Art, Boulder, CO, January 2002.

Flippin, Royce. "Slow Down You Breathe Too Fast." *American Health* (June 1992), pp. 74–75.

Gass, Robert. *Chanting: Discovering Spirit in Sound.* NY: Broadway Books, 1999.

"Improving Employee Productivity: Encourage Proper Breathing." *Business Journal of New Jersey* 8 (Annual, 1990), p. S32.

Khalsa, Dharma Singh, and Cameron Stauth. *Meditation as Medicine: Activate the Power of Your Natural Healing Force.* NY: Pocket Books, 2001.

Loehr, Jim, with Susan Festa Fiske. "Breathe Your Way to Better Play." *Tennis* 30 (December 1994), p. 61.

"Mind in Body Building: Breathe Deeply for the Body and the Mind." *Muscle and Fitness* 54 (October 1993), p. 73. Reprint from the University of Texas Life Time Health Letter.

Sky, Michael. *Breathing: Expanding Your Power and Energy.* NM: Bear and Company Publishing, 1990.

Sung, B. H., O. Roussanov, M. Nagvbandi, and L. Golden. "Effectiveness of Various Relaxation Techniques in Lowering Blood Pressure Associated with Mental Stress." *American Journal of Hypertension* 13 (2000), pp. 185A–186A.

Zi, Nancy. *The Art of Breathing.* NY: Bantam Books, 1986.

Chapter 5: Yoga

A'nanda Ma'rga. *Teaching Asanas: An A'nanda Ma'rga Manual for Teachers.* CA: Amrit Publications, 1973.

Bramlett, Wendy, Director. Yoga Instruction at Studio Be, Boulder, CO, 2002.

Gaudoin, Tina. "Yoga: Mystical Goes Mainstream." *Harper's Bazaar* (October 1992), p. 206 (3 p.).

Hittleman, Richard. *Yoga 28 Day Exercise Plan*. NY: Workman Publishing, 1969.

Kallenbach, Laurel. "Why Yoga Works When Diets Often Fail." *Yoga Journal* (November/December 2000), p. 78 (12 p.).

Radha, Swami Sivanada. *Hatha Yoga: The Hidden Language*. MA: Shambhala, 1989.

Rattenbury, Jeanne. "Yoga for Total Fitness." *Vegetarian Times* (September 1993), p. 67 (5 p.).

Satchidananda, Yogiraj Sri Swami. *Integral Yoga Hatha*. NY: Holt, Rinehart and Winston, 1970.

Yee, Rodney, with Nina Zolotow. *Yoga: The Poetry of the Body*. NY: St. Martin's Griffin, 2002.

Yogananda, Paramahansa. *Autobiography of a Yogi*. CA: Self-Realization Fellowship, 1977.

Chapter 6: The Mind

Buscaglia, Leo. *Love*. NY: Ballantine Books, 1972.

Carpi, John. "Stress, It's Worse Than You Think." *Psychology Today* (January/February 1996), p. 34 (10 p.).

Cousins, Norman. *Anatomy of an Illness, as Perceived by the Patient*. NY: W.W. Norton, 1979.

Deam, Jenny. "In Prozac We Trust." *Denver Post*, July 11, 2000.

Gawain, Shakti. *Creative Visualization*. CA: Whatever Publishing, 1978.

Hay, Louise L. *You Can Heal Your Life*. CA: Hay House, 1984.

Health Resource Network, Inc. "Stress Facts." Web site, www.stresscure.com, 1999.

Heller, Diane Poole, with Laurence S. Heller. *Crash Course: A Self-Healing Guide to Auto Accident Trauma and Recovery*. CA: North Atlantic Books, 2001.

King, Serge. *Kahuna Healing*. IL: Theosophical Publishing House, 1983.

Laura, Ronald S. "Not Just for Laughs." *Muscle and Fitness* 53 (December 1992), pp. 148–227.

Levine, Peter, with Ann Frederick. *Waking the Tiger: Healing Trauma.* CA: North Atlantic Books, 1997.

Penfield, Wilder. *Mystery of the Mind: A Critical Study of Consciousness and the Human Brain.* NJ: Princeton University Press, 1976.

Pert, Candace B. *Molecules of Emotion: Why You Feel the Way You Feel.* NY: Scribner, 1997.

Sare, Chris. "A Joy to Be Held." *Muscle and Fitness* 53 (October 1992), p. 48.

Scaer, Robert C. *The Body Bears the Burden: Trauma, Dissociation, and Disease.* NY: Haworth Medical Press, 2001.

Stark, Elizabeth. "Stress." *American Health* (December 1992), p. 41 (7 p.).

University of Iowa College of Medicine. "Stress and Your Heart: Facts and Statistics." Web site, www.vh.org, 1999.

Chapter 7: Meditation

Adair, Margo. *Working Inside Out: Tools for Change.* CA: Wingbow Press, 1984.

Dass, Ram. *Journey of Awakening: A Meditator's Guidebook.* NY: Bantam Books, 1990.

Edy, Carolyn. "No Side Effects." *Yoga Journal* (October 2000), p. 37.

Fontana, David. *The Elements of Meditation.* MA: Element, 1991.

Gass, Robert. *Chanting: Discovering Spirit in Sound.* NY: Broadway Books, 1999.

Harp, David. *The Three Minute Meditator.* CA: New Harbinger Publications, 1996.

Kabat-Zinn, Jon. *Wherever You Go There You Are: Mindfulness Meditation in Everyday Life.* NY: Hyperion, 1994.

Khalsa, Dharma Singh, and Cameron Stauth. *Meditation as Medicine: Activate the Power of Your Natural Healing Force.* NY: Pocket Books, 2001.

Reder, Alan. "Take a Seat." *Yoga Journal* (February 2001), pp. 106–111.

Chapter 8: Chakras

Anderson, Bob. *Stretching.* CA: Shelter Publications, 1980.

Avalon, Arthur. *The Serpent Power.* NY: Dover Publications, 1974.

Brennan, Barbara Ann. *Hands of Light.* NY: Bantam Books, 1987.

Bruyere, Rosalyn L. *Wheels of Light: A Study of the Chakras.* CA: Bon Productions, 1989.

Halpern, Steven, with Louis Savary. *Sound Health: The Music and Sounds That Make Us Whole.* CA: Harper and Row, 1985.

Judith, Anodea. *The Chakra System: A Complete Course in Self-Diagnosis and Healing.* CO: Sounds True, 2000. Audiocassette.

Judith, Anodea. *Eastern Body, Western Mind: Psychology and the Chakra System as a Path to the Self.* CA: Celestial Arts, 1996.

Judith, Anodea. *Wheels of Life: A User's Guide to the Chakras.* MN: Llewellyn Publications, 1987.

Myss, Caroline. *Anatomy of the Spirit: The Seven Stages of Power and Healing.* NY: Tree River Press, 1996.

Yogananda, Paramahansa. *Autobiography of a Yogi.* CA: Self-Realization Fellowship, 1977.

Chapter 9: Angels, Devas, and Spirits of the Earth

Burnham, Sophy. *A Book of Angels: Reflections on Angels Past and Present and True Stories of How They Touch Our Lives.* NY: Ballantine Books, 1990.

Burnham, Sophy. "The Joy of Angels." *Ladies Home Journal* (December 1994), pp. 102–176.

Castro, Peter, Tom Gliatto, and Samantha Miller. "Angels in America." *People Weekly* 48, no. 25 (December 1997), p. 78 (6 p.).

Dossey, Larry. "Prayer: Old Approach, New Wonders." *The Quest* (summer 1990), p. 36.

Freeman, Eileen Elias. *Touched by Angels.* NY: Warner Books, 1993.

Gauldie, Enid P. "Flights of Angels." *History Today* 42 (December 1992), pp. 13–20.

Gibbs, Nancy. "Angels Among Us." *Time* (December 1993), p. 56.

Gross, Andrea. "I Met an Angel." *Ladies Home Journal* (December 1992), p. 60.

Hall, Manley P. *The Secret Teachings of All Ages.* CA: Philosophical Research Society, 1988.

Harner, Michael. *The Way of the Shaman.* NY: Bantam Books, 1980.

Highwater, Jamake, and Alfred Van Der Marck. *The Rituals of the Wind.* NY: Editions, 1984.

Howard, Jane M. *Commune with the Angels: A Heavenly Handbook*. VA: A.R.E. Press, 1992.

Kuthumi. *Studies of the Human Aura*. CA: Summit University Press, 1971.

Looking Horse, Chief Arvol. *White Buffalo Teachings*. MA: Dreamkeepers Press, 2001.

Starck, Marcia. *Women's Medicine Ways*. CA: Crossing Press, 1993.

Taylor, Terry Lynn. *Guardians of Hope: The Angels' Guide to Personal Growth*. CA: H. J. Kramer, 1992.

Williamson, Duncan. *The Broonies, Silkies and Fairies: Travellers' Tales of the Other World*. NY: Harmony Books, 1985.

Chapter 10: Prayer and Positive Thoughts

Benson, Herbert, with Mary Stark. *Timeless Healing*. NY: Scribner, 1996.

Bernardi L., P. Sleight, G. Bandinelli, S. Cencetti, L. Fattorini, J. Wdowczyc-Szulc, and A. Lagi. "Effect of Rosary Prayer and Yoga Mantras on Autonomic Cardiovascular Rhythms: Comparative Study." *British Medical Journal* 323 (2001), pp. 1446–1449.

Daniel, Alma, Timothy Wyllie, and Andrew Kamer. *Ask Your Angels*. NY: Ballantine Books, 1992.

Dossey, Larry. *Healing Words: The Power of Prayer and the Practice of Medicine*. CA: HarperSanFrancisco, 1993.

Dossey, Larry. *Recovering the Soul: A Scientific and Spiritual Search*. NY: Bantam Books, 1989.

Gallia, Katherine, Susanne Althoff, and Melissa Nachatelo. "Power of Prayer." *Natural Health* 29, no. 3 (April 1999), p. 34.

King, Serge. *The Aloha Spirit*. CA: Huna International, n.d.

Markides, Kyriacos C. *Fire in the Heart*. NY: Paragon House, 1990.

McCarthy, Laura Flynn. "Prayer's Power over Your Heart." *Better Nutrition* 64, no. 2 (February 2002), p. S6.

Munson, Marty, with Teresa Yeykal. "Brain Against Pain." *Prevention* (January 1996), p. 50.

Stenddal-Rast, David. *The Grateful Heart*. CO: Sounds True, 1992. Audioassette.

Van Biema, David. "Faith and Healing." *Time* (June 24, 1996), p. 59 (9 p.).

Mary Capone   *Janet Rupp*

About the Authors

Mary Capone is a writer and a founding member of the School of Sound and Sacred Art, as well as a long-time practitioner of yoga, sound, breath, aromatherapy, meditation, and more. For the last 10 years, Ms. Capone has apprenticed with many energy work masters and applies many of the valuable techniques discussed in the book in her daily practice.

Janet Rupp is an internationally known hands-on healer who has maintained a beloved private non-traditional therapy practice for 20 years. Her multi-cultural practice is based on studies with Lakota Elders, Mayan shamans, psychic healers, a New Mexican Curandero as well as many U.S. masters of energy work. She is certified in acupuncture, herbal medicine, color analysis, iridology, hands-on healing, astrology and as a healing minister.